AC
Two-litre Saloons &
Buckland Sports cars

Including a performance tuning guide for the AC two-litre engine

"There is hardly anything in the world that some man cannot make a little worse and so a little cheaper, and the people who consider price only are this man's lawful prey"

(John Ruskin)

Other Veloce publications -

Colour Family Album Series

Alfa Romeo by Andrea & David Sparrow
Bubblecars & Microcars by Andrea & David Sparrow
Bubblecars & Microcars, More by Andrea & David Sparrow
Citroen 2CV by Andrea & David Sparrow
Citroen DS by Andrea & David Sparrow
Custom VWs by Andrea & David Sparrow
Fiat & Abarth 500 & 600 by Andrea & David Sparrow
Lambretta by Andrea & David Sparrow
Mini & Mini Cooper by Andrea & David Sparrow
Motor Scooters by Andrea & David Sparrow
Porsche by Andrea & David Sparrow
Triumph Sportscars by Andrea & David Sparrow
Vespa by Andrea & David Sparrow
VW Beetle by Andrea & David Sparrow
VW Bus, Camper, Van & Pick-up by Andrea & David Sparrow
VW Custom Beetle by Andrea & David Sparrow

SpeedPro Series

How to Blueprint & Build a 4-Cylinder Engine Short Block for High Performance by Des Hammill
How to Build a V8 Engine Short Block for High Performance by Des Hammill
How to Plan and Build a Fast Road Car by Daniel Stapleton
How to Build & Modify Sportscar/Kitcar Suspension & Brakes by Des Hammill
How to Build & Modify SU Carburettors for High Performance by Des Hammill
How to Build & Power Tune Weber DCOE & Dellorto DHLA Carburetors Second Edition by Des Hammill
How to Build & Power Tune Harley-Davidson Evolution Engines by Des Hammill
How to Build & Power Tune Distributor-type Ignition Systems by Des Hammill
How to Build, Modify & Power Tune Cylinder Heads Second Edition by Peter Burgess
How to Build Your Own Tiger Avon Sportscar by Jim Dudley
How to Choose Camshafts & Time them for Maximum Power by Des Hammill
How to Give your MGB V8 Power Updated & Revised Edition by Roger Williams
How to Improve the MGB, MGC & MGB V8 by Roger Williams
How to Modify Volkswagen Beetle Chassis, Suspension & Brakes for High Performance by James Hale
How to Power Tune Mini Engines on a Small Budget by Des Hammill
How to Power Tune the BMC 998cc A-Series Engine by Des Hammill
How to Power Tune BMC/Rover 1275cc A-Series Engines by Des Hammill
How to Power Tune the MGB 4-Cylinder Engine by Peter Burgess
How to Power Tune the MG Midget & Austin-Healey Sprite Updated Edition by Daniel Stapleton
How to Power Tune Alfa Romeo Twin Cam Engines by Jim Kartalamakis
How to Power Tune Ford SOHC 'Pinto' & Sierra Cosworth DOHC Engines Updated & Revised Edition by Des Hammill
How to Power Tune Jaguar XK Engines by Des Hammill
How to Power Tune Rover V8 Engines by Des Hammill

General

AC Two-litre Saloons & Buckand Sportscars by Leo Archibald
Alfa Romeo Berlinas (Saloons/Sedans) by John Tipler
Alfa Romeo Giulia Coupe GT & GTA by John Tipler
Anatomy of the Works Minis by Brian Moylan
Automotive A-Z, Lane's Dictionary of Automotive Terms by Keith Lane
Automotive Mascots by David Kay & Lynda Springate
Bentley Continental, Corniche and Azure, by Martin Bennett
BMW 5-Series by Marc Cranswick
BMW Z-Cars by James Taylor
British Cars, The Complete Catalogue of, 1895-1975 by Culshaw & Horrobin
British Police Cars by Nick Walker
British Trailer Caravans 1919-1959 by Andrew Jenkinson

British Trailer Caravans from 1960 by Andrew Jenkinson
Bugatti Type 40 by Barrie Price
Bugatti 46/50 Updated Edition by Barrie Price
Bugatti 57 2nd Edition - by Barrie Price
Caravanning & Trailer Tenting, the Essential Handbook by Len Archer
Chrysler 300 - America's Most Powerful Car by Robert Ackerson
Cobra - The Real Thing! by Trevor Legate
Cortina - Ford's Bestseller by Graham Robson
Daimler SP250 'Dart' by Brian Long
Datsun/Nissan 280ZX & 300ZX by Brian Long
Datsun Z - From Fairlady to 280Z by Brian Long
Dune Buggy Handbook by James Hale
Fiat & Abarth 124 Spider & Coupe by John Tipler
Fiat & Abarth 500 & 600 by Malcolm Bobbitt
Ford F100/F150 Pick-up by Robert Ackerson
Ford GT40 by Trevor Legate
Ford Model Y by Sam Roberts
Harley-Davidson, Growing up by Jean Davidson
Jaguar XJ-S, by Brian Long
Karmann-Ghia Coupe & Convertible by Malcolm Bobbitt
Land Rover, The Half-Ton Military by Mark Cook
Lea-Francis Story, The by Barrie Price
Lexus Story, The by Brian Long
Lola - The Illustrated History (1957-1977) by John Starkey
Lola - All The Sports Racing & Single-Seater Racing Cars 1978-1997 by John Starkey
Lola T70 - The Racing History & Individual Chassis Record 3rd Edition by John Starkey
Lotus 49 by Michael Oliver
Mazda MX-5/Miata 1.6 Enthusiast's Workshop Manual by Rod Grainger & Pe Shoemark
Mazda MX-5/Miata 1.8 Enthusiast's Workshop Manual by Rod Grainger & Pe Shoemark
Mazda MX-5 (& Eunos Roadster) - The World's Favourite Sportscar by Brian Long
MGA by John Price Williams
MGB & MGB GT - Expert Guide (Auto-Doc Series) by Roger Williams
Mini Cooper - The Real Thing! by John Tipler
Mitsubishi Lancer Evo by Brian Long
Motor Racing at Goodwood in the Sixties by Tony Gardiner
MR2 - Toyota's Mid-engined Sports Car by Brian Long
Porsche 356 by Brian Long
Porsche 911R, RS & RSR, 4th Ed. by John Starkey
Porsche 914 & 914-6 by Brian Long
Porsche 924 by Brian Long
Porsche 944 by Brian Long
Rolls-Royce Silver Shadow/Bentley T Series Corniche & Camargue Updated Editic by Malcolm Bobbitt
Rolls-Royce Silver Spirit, Silver Spur & Bentley Mulsanne by Malcolm Bobbitt
Rolls-Royce Silver Wraith, Dawn & Cloud/Bentley MkVI, R & S Series by Martyn Nutland
RX-7 - Mazda's Rotary Engine Sportscar by Brian Long
Singer Story: Cars, Commercial Vehicles, Bicycles & Motorcycles by Kevin Atkinson
Taxi! The Story of the 'London' Taxicab by Malcolm Bobbitt
Triumph Motorcycles & the Meriden Factory by Hughie Hancox
Triumph Tiger Cub Bible by Mike Estall
Triumph Trophy Bible by Harry Woolridge
Triumph TR2/3/3A, How to Restore, by Roger Williams
Triumph TR4/4A, How to Restore, by Roger Williams
Triumph TR5/250 & 6, How to Restore, by Roger Williams
Triumph TR6 by William Kimberley
Turner's Triumphs, Edward Turner & his Triumph Motorcycles by Jeff Clew
Velocette Motorcycles - MSS to Thruxton by Rod Burris
Volkswagens of the World by Simon Glen
VW Beetle Cabriolet by Malcolm Bobbitt
VW Beetle - The Car of the 20th Century by Richard Copping
VW Bus, Camper, Van, Pickup by Malcolm Bobbitt
Works Rally Mechanic by Brian Moylan

First published in 2002 by Veloce Publishing Ltd., 33, Trinity Street, Dorchester DT1 1TT, England. Fax: 01305 268864/e-mail: info@veloce.co.uk website: www.veloce.co.uk
ISBN: 1-903706-24-6/UPC: 36847-00224-4. Leather edition ISBN: 1-903706-71-8/UPC: 36847-00271-8

Readers with ideas for automotive books, or books on other transport or related hobby subjects, are invited to write to Veloce Publishing at the abov address.
British Library Cataloguing in Publication Data -
A catalogue record for this book is available from the British Library.
Typesetting (Bookman), design and page make-up all by Veloce on AppleMac.
Printed and bound in the EC.

AC
Two-litre Saloons &
Buckland Sports cars

Including a performance tuning guide for the AC two-litre engine

– Leo Archibald –

VELOCE PUBLISHING
THE PUBLISHER OF FINE AUTOMOTIVE BOOKS

Publisher's Note
Some of the illustrations in this book have been scanned from poor quality originals: these images have nevertheless been included because of their rarity and to add to the completeness to this work.

CONTENTS

PREFACE, ACKNOWLEDGEMENTS & ABOUT THE AUTHOR

I am delighted to know that at last there is to be a record of my late husband's involvement with AC Cars.

This period of our lives was very full. Ernie was busy with several business enterprises, the farm and the family involvement with Covent Garden Market as well as the creation of his dream car, the AC Buckland Tourer. Although I did not get involved with the practicalities of the cars, being busy raising our 4 lovely daughters, I did get to enjoy all the 'test drives', competing in the Concours d'Elegance at Brighton and our holidays to the South of France, and of course our annual visit to the Motor Show. I was also able to help with the photo shoots as you will see.

I hope that readers of this book will find the history of interest, it has brought many happy memories flooding back to me.

Joan Bailey

Joan Bailey

Royston, Herts

May 2001

PREFACE

When the Second World War ended, AC restarted car production with a new sports saloon. The company expected sales to be brisk, and they were. In fact, the factory produced nearly 1300 cars, and the revenue allowed AC to further develop the two-litre engine. This meant that when the company had the opportunity to produce the AC Ace sports car in 1954, the engine was ready to be dropped into the new Ace chassis. It's probable, therefore, that without the production success of the Two-litre saloon, with more of these cars being produced than any other AC car since the 1920s, including the mighty Cobra, the AC Ace/Cobra might never have come to fruition!

ACKNOWLEDGEMENTS

I would first of all like to thank all those who have written about and photographed the AC car through the years, maintaining the interest in, and increasing the understanding of, the diversity of the AC Marque. I would also like to thank the AC Owners Club, AC Cars and the National Motor Museum, Beaulieu, for the supply of photographs and detailed information

Leo Archibald at the wheel of his very successful road/racing special. The picture was taken in 1986 at one of the Galway hill climb events.

without which this book could not have been produced.

Special thanks go to Joan Bailey and Angela Louch who have loaned me their priceless family photographs of Ernie Bailey and the Buckland Body Works (many of these photos never before published). Thanks, too, to Pete Mercer of AC Cars for his assistance and tireless work in producing the chassis number records.

Ron Clayton, John Tojeiro and Joan Clarke, all past employees of the Buckland Body Works, were always on hand to offer assistance. Thanks, too, to Tony Cutting for the use of his lovely white Two-litre for many of the photos. Graham White, Tom Dine and John McClelland of the AC Club helped provide invaluable information and archive material. Thanks to Motor Racing Publications for the use of photos, and to Brian Gilbart-Smith for his enthusiasm for this project and the loan of pictures of early saloons.

My thanks must also go to Alan Turner and Keith Judd, ex-employees of AC Cars: Alan for his insight into the design of the Two-litre, in which he had a large part; and Keith for his recollections of his early days at AC Cars.

Rod Briggs provided the AC engine photos, Kevin Quinlan loaned the photos of his beautiful 1949 Drophead Two-litre, Ian Strange allowed the inclusion of some of his Two-litre ash framing diagrams, Simon Taylor and *Autocar* supplied an early Two-litre cutaway drawing, Mike Smith helped

in the hunt for Buckland material and Stuart Wallace provided AC drawings. I extend my gratitude to you all.

David Meynell, my long time friend and AC companion (sadly no longer with us), spent endless hours with me discussing the merits of certain AC designs and how they could be improved upon. Bill Bailey and Graham Portwine gave up their valuable time to help me track down photos and information for the book. Ian Archibald, my brother, initially sparked my interest in AC cars by purchasing and bringing home the first Two-litre AC I had seen. I would also like to thank my friends Brian Woodward, whose engineering excellence has kept many Spitfires in the air, and Betty Woodward for her patience in copying so many amended drawings.

A special thank you to my wife Resa for her time and patience. Thanks also to Joe Boyle for his enthusiasm, understanding and for generally being a good friend over the years and helping me put this book together. Finally I would like to thank Allison Bennett,

Andrea Robinson and Karen Whittaker, whose patience in interpreting my handwriting and putting this through a keyboard into print was invaluable.

ABOUT THE AUTHOR

Leo built his own AC special in the late 1970s with a view to using the car in historic racing and as a sports car for ordinary road use.

He campaigned his AC Special in the 1980s racing mainly in Ireland at Mondelo Park Motor Racing Circuit, Naas, the famous Phoenix Park races and several hillclimb venues, his favourite being the Cork Screw and the Ballyallaban hillclimbs south of Galway, both in the region of two miles long. It was the AC's reliability rather than outright speed that clocked up the points to win the Irish Historic Championship Class outright in 1988, as well as a first at the Bentley Drivers Club race meeting at Silverstone in 1986.

Today, Leo lives in the north of England and continues to drive and restore AC cars.

1

A BRIEF INTRODUCTION TO AC CARS

The story of the AC Car Company goes back to 1901, when a very talented design engineer, John Weller, met and received the financial backing of a prosperous and astute South London businessman, John Portwine. Portwine had a string of butchers' shops in London and, just as the AC Car Company is still producing cars over a hundred years later, there is still a butcher's shop in Covent Garden with the name Portwine over the door. It is run by Graham Portwine, a relative of John.

AC's first production motor vehicle, named the Auto-Carrier, was a timber framed three-wheeled vehicle with an air-cooled single-cylinder 636cc engine. The design called for two wheels at the front and one at the rear. The engine was placed in front of the rear wheel under the driver's seat. Steering the AC was carried out by a tiller, and a large capacity carrying box was placed between the front wheels.

The Auto-Carrier went into production in 1904 and was an immediate success, with most of the

A number of vehicles on display in AC's showroom in 1913. (Courtesy AC Owners Club)

The first type of Auto-Carrier built.

The later 1909 Auto-Carrier with the passenger in front of the driver.

large department stores purchasing them. Speed, reliability and ease of maintenance were the key elements. They sold for £85 and were a very common sight on the London roads.

A passenger variant was introduced in 1907. Initially, this still had the driver sitting over the engine with the passenger in the front. The design was quickly modified, however, and the passenger and driver sat beside each other. In 1910, several Auto-Carriers were supplied to the military for carrying arms, ammunition and soldiers.

Although production of the Auto-Carriers continued, Weller had begun working on the design of a four-wheeled car. This was ready in 1913, but no

The 1910 version of the Auto-Carrier can be seen here in the middle. The vehicle was aptly called the AC Sociable, and no, the driver is not the well known silent film comic.

The Auto-Carrier in use with the military in 1910.

Probably the first four-wheeled AC built. This photo was taken in 1913.

This picture, taken in 1921, shows the founders of AC Cars John Weller, left, and John Portwine.

progress was really made until after the 1914-18 war. The first four-wheeled cars were powered by French Fivet engines but, when the supply of these was exhausted, the Anzani four-cylinder 11.8hp was introduced. In fact, this proved so popular that all Anzani production was taken over by AC.

Through 1918 John Weller was working on his design for a very light two-litre six-cylinder engine which was publicly announced in 1919, but was slow to get into production. By 1923, however, the design was well sorted and featured an aluminium block and sump, with steel liners for the cylinders. For its time this engine was extremely light and gave plenty of power. This power unit would remain in production, with various beneficial modifications taking place, of course, right through to 1963.

In 1921, S.F. Edge took over control of the company and John Weller and John Portwine resigned. Throughout the 1920s, AC produced a variety of models all fitted with the combined rear axle and gearbox which gave three forward gears and one

An AC four-seater in 1922.

The first of the six-cylinder two-seaters

The Saloon in 1929, with high-type radiator.

A very attractive four-seat drophead Coupé from 1936. (Courtesy AC Owners Club)

reverse, the final drive being by worm and wormwheel. Although the axle was light, it became noisy when worn, and soon became unpopular.

Although the company had a great deal of success throughout the 1920s, setting many motoring records along the way, with the start of the great

A 1930s AC Sports, racing at Silverstone in the 1950s. (Courtesy AC Owners Club)

AC excelled in making beautiful tourers in the 1930s and this car is no exception. (Courtesy AC Owners Club)

depression in 1929 things were looking very bleak. Financial difficulties ultimately caused AC to cease car production and the company went into receivership.

The Hurlock family took control of AC at the start of the Thirties, and produced a succession of beautiful two- and four-seater sports cars, along with saloons and dropheads, throughout the decade. The factory continued with the development of the AC engine and standardised the triple SU carburettor set-up. Power rose from the 40bhp of the early engines to 80bhp in the late Thirties. There were also a few special supercharged engines which produced 90bhp!

By 1939, the competition from other manufacturers was beginning to tell, and sales of new ACs were slowing dramatically. The Hurlocks knew something very different was needed, but the 1939-45 war was about to commence and any fresh ideas were put on hold. Throughout 1939 to 1945, AC concentrated on the war effort, producing fire engines, aircraft undercarriages and guns, and any other machining work that it could undertake.

When the war was over, AC designers began planning a new model. With the experience of metallurgy and streamlining gained during the war years, things would never be the same again.

The 1937 Aero Saloon. (Courtesy AC Owners Club)

H. Fry with his 1938 fixed head Coupé. (Courtesy AC Owners Club)

Owner Leslie Stephenson with his 1938 drophead. (Courtesy AC Owners Club)

2

THE IDEA BEHIND THE AC TWO-LITRE SALOON

In the austere period following the second world war, it became apparent to the directors of AC Cars that the company needed to produce a practical and reliable car, with at least the pretence of being sporty. Thus the Two-litre (Sports) Saloon was born.

The standard of the day was for a low, sleek, well built car with adequate performance. This was just what the public wanted, and production of the Two-litre saloon was to be in the region of 5 to 10 cars per week. Incidentally, this car and its variants outsold the 1950s Aces and Acecas, and also the mighty Cobra of the 'sixties.

The cars were built in the traditional AC fashion: a rigid separate chassis onto which four half-elliptic springs (cart springs) were fitted. These actually did their job very well, the front springs sliding in trunnions at their rear ends, while the rear springs still retained swinging shackles. It was old-fashioned but, with longer and wider springs than the 1939 chassis, plus the new telescopic shock absorbers at the front and lever arm shock absorbers at the rear, a four speed gearbox and separate back axle, the chassis was well received and gave the car the very steady handling characteristics AC was looking for.

A light ashwood frame clothed with an aluminium body was bolted onto the chassis, and the interior was finished in high quality leather, bound carpets and polished timber dashboard and door cappings. Underneath the bonnet was the trusted and reliable, though by now long in the tooth, AC six-cylinder two-litre engine, with the modified water pump now positioned at the side of the engine block allowing a lower bonnet line.

The company's plan was to build a high quality, single model car at a competitive price (AC's aim in 1946 was to keep the price under £1000, plus purchase tax). The total price, inclusive of purchase tax, was £1277.

The price did rise over the years, of course, and competition again became fierce, but more of this later.

By 1947, the designers at AC had the basic shape of the model looking just about right, within the constraints of keeping development costs down and changes to a minimum. The designers of the Two-litre, Alan Turner and Z. Marcewski, were at pains to retain a solid reliability for the car, careful detailing to a tried and tested concept was the order of the day. The 'newfangled' independent front suspension system, for example, was deemed inappropriate as it could lead to major development time and still not prove satisfactory . So a beam axle was retained at the front combined with a conventional rigid rear axle.

The next few years saw many body styles being introduced, such as the open Buckland Sports, AC's own drophead, a four-door version, and a few special bodied cars.

The Hurlocks were very conservative, however, and always wary of costs impinging on profit. They probably thought that the styling of the new model should be a compromise between the old 'thirties-styled illustrations and the very modern Riley Pathfinder, and thus the definitive Two-litre shape was decided on.

A total of 1286 chassis were produced in the end: 1107 were designated as two-door saloons; 90 were Buckland and similar AC Sports Tourers; 48 were four-door cars; 14 were drophead coupés; 1 was a special convertible; and a final 26 chassis were sent to specialist coachbuilders for estate and sports bodies to be built. In fact, if it wasn't for the large production run, by AC's standards, and the development of the AC engine while the saloons were being built, the AC Ace sports car of 1954/55 might not have been built.

W.A.E. Hurlock.

3

THE HEART OF THE TWO-LITRE SALOON, THE AC TWO-LITRE ENGINE

Much has already been written about this superb engine, so what follows here is merely intended as a review. Designed by the brilliant engineer John Weller, it was introduced in 1919 to a very enthusiastic motor trade and public alike.

Although the six-cylinder engine looks archaic today, with its bore and stroke of 65mm x 100mm, it was very advanced for the period and gave a very smooth power band. The block, sump and valve chest cover were all produced in aluminium, thus minimising weight. Six separate steel liners were fitted into the block, and gaskets were used to prohibit water from entering the crankcase. The six pistons and conrods were attached to a sturdy crankshaft which was held in

place in the block by four main bearings. By 1926, though, the number of main bearings had been increased to five, the fifth being positioned close to the flywheel. The oil pump was fitted low in the sump and provided excellent oil distribution. A cast iron cross flow cylinder head was fitted on top of the engine, with the camshaft fitting snugly under the overhead valve gear.

Weller's idea was to drive the camshaft using a chain from the crankshaft. Unfortunately, using such a long chain meant that it thrashed around in the crankcase to an unacceptable extent. The solution to this problem was so simple in engineering terms that Weller's invention, which he patented, was widely adopted and made him a wealthy

The Two-litre AC engine and gearbox as fitted to the saloons and Bucklands. This picture shows the drive for the rev counter at the base of the distributor. The whole engine design looks very attractive.

The bottom end of an early post-war engine showing the split flywheel bolted together with rubber bushes acting as torsional dampers.

The bottom end of a later engine showing the solid flywheel and the torsional damper fitted to the front of the crankshaft. The cross-shaft drive gear can be seen near the rear of the crankshaft, and you can also see the main bearing oil supply gallery pipes.

Reprinted by kind permission
of the "Autocar"

*Here the camshaft is clearly visible
sitting under the rocker gear, as is
the chain-driven timing sprocket on
the right, and the triple SU
carburettors and their inlet
manifolds.*

An excellent sectional drawing by Max Miller from Autocar showing the low chassis, under-slung at the rear, and the basic layout of the chassis and main components.

nan. His design patent was for a simple spring steel slipper tensioner which he chain could rest against, thus keeping it taut and quiet at all times.

In the early 'twenties, with its ready CR (compression ratio) of 5.25:1, he engine produced 40bhp, giving an excellent power to weight ratio in relation to other contemporary power units. The phrase "The world's finest ight six" was coined, and was used by the company in its advertising material well into the 1950s.

Development was steady throughout the 'twenties and, in the 'thirties, triple carburettors became the norm. Roller camshaft followers were also used, and top end cam noise was reduced by the introduction of an eccentric-base camshaft. The water pump was bolted directly in front of the camshaft. White metal bearings were used on both the main and big end bearings, and, by the end of the 'thirties, the engine was regarded as very reliable, with more than adequate power.

The engine's Achilles heel, however, was its long stroke which restricted maximum safe revs to 4500rpm. Also, compression ratios could not be significantly raised because conrod bearing failure could occur as a consequence.

The flywheel was modified by being split into two halves, with six rubber mouldings between the two parts to facilitate the flywheel acting as a torsional damper for the crankshaft. Crankshaft vibration wasn't completely cured, but it was subdued to an acceptable level.

In 1946 it was decided that the water pump should be relocated to the side of the engine. This allowed for a much lower bonnet line and improved the flow of water through the block and radiator. Larger valves were fitted, and bronze-backed white metal shell-type main bearings were introduced. The conrods retained plain white metal bearings, though, since these were regarded as more than adequate for use with a compression ratio of 6.5:1 (which, by this time, could be regarded as low). However, the combination of these big-end bearings and the long stroke meant that the engine didn't welcome high revolutions, and it was 'redlined' at 4500rpm. With the development of the Ace sports car, though, more power was needed and standard shell-type bearings were fitted to the big-ends, allowing a compression ratio of 8.0:1. These shell bearing engines were also fitted in later saloons.

A gear situated near the rear of the crankshaft turned a cross-shaft which drove the dynamo and distributor.

The post-war car was fitted with triple $1^1/_8$ inch SU carburettors which gave smooth running and good economy. They rather strangled top end performance, though, and, as with the Ace, $1^1/_4$ inch SUs could be fitted to give more power through the rev range and at the top end.

Although the engine block was still cast in aluminium, corrosion, which was a major problem in the 'twenties and 'thirties, had been virtually eliminated by the use of higher quality aluminium casting material. The engine weighed in the region of 350lb in this specification and looked very attractive. It was tall, slender and very purposeful-looking with its triple carb set-up. When ordering the car many clients would specify the polished aluminium rocker cover and carburettors (at extra cost, of course). This was indeed a car to show off to your friends.

A personal friend of the author remembers driving his boss's Two-litre saloon in the mid-'fifties. In fact, he recalls the experience as if it was yesterday. The car was smooth, taut, fast, had fabulous road holding, and was a car to both be seen in and to take pride in owning.

Sadly, in recent years, many people have judged the performance of Two-litre cars by unknowingly driving examples with worn suspension and tired engines: such cars make a very poor comparison to those with healthy suspension and well-tuned engines.

4

THE EARLY DESIGN, PRODUCTION AND DEVELOPMENT OF THE TWO-LITRE SALOON

In April 1946, with longer and wider springs and new shock absorbers, compared to the pre-war chassis design, the first newly designed post-war experimental Two-litre chassis (L800) was registered. A pre-war drophead body was placed on the new chassis for testing in the UK and on the Continent.

It soon became apparent that the concept of fitting wider and longer springs, whilst retaining beam axles both front and rear, and utilising modern shock absorbers on a very strong crossbraced chassis, worked very well. The chassis was strengthened with box sections where necessary and the improved water pump layout and radiator circulation system worked commendably well. Hydro-mechanical brakes, which required relatively heavy pedal pressures, completed the package.

The chassis and suspension and gave excellent road holding and a comfortable, if rather stiff ride over most surfaces. The ride only became uncomfortable on rough, bumpy surfaces where the suspension could be found wanting.

The bonnet was initially hinged at the rear and was opened by pulling on a lever at the front of the bonnet. This system was felt to be too complicated, however, and all production cars were fitted with a centrally hinged bonnet. Wire mesh stone guards were fitted under each wing to protect the aluminium from stone chips. This was a nice touch, and these wire guards remained a standard feature on the AC Saloon throughout its production run.

It appears that at this time, in 1946, even though the AC car production records don't show it, AC purchased two Alvis TA14 chassis, numbers 21130 and 21307, from Alvis distributors Brooklands of Bond Street (Alvis records detail the purchase). Woody estate bodies were then built on these chassis and fitted for supply to Fairey Aviation in 1947. Quite why AC didn't use its own chassis isn't clear, though it does appear that AC built at least one Woody on its own chassis, but no AC records of this car or cars seem to exist.

No doubt the engineers at Thames Ditton crawled all over the Alvis chassis to assess the workings and merits of their design. It should be mentioned at this time that it's not clear whether the Woody bodies were built by AC or by Ernie Bailey's Buckland Body Works, since Buckland had built two or three such cars at this time.

With road testing well underway, the factory set about building the prototype saloon, chassis number L801, which was registered at the beginning of 1947. An early concept design model showed a remarkable resemblance to the Jaguar XK120 in its lines (very sleek and low). However, for whatever reason, this design was not put into practice on the production car. Early drawings of the car released to the motoring press gave an idea as to what AC was trying to achieve in both saloon and drophead forms. Many of the ideas presented in these drawings were put into practice on the production model, including neater detailing to the headlights, for example.

An early artist's impression, three quarter rear view, of how he felt the new saloon should look. It was probably drawn in early 1946 along with the other pictures. Note the number plate model designation of ACE 1947.

Initial progress was swift, and sixteen cars left the factory during 1947, with changes being made almost on a car by car basis. Early cars, for example, had the trafficators set low on the car's side panel behind the doors. These were then moved to behind the rear side windows. The rear wheel spats were dropped, as was the piece of timber used to cover the headlining seam near the rear of the car. The latter was well made, of course, with intricate bends and angles: it was also stained and polished, and being over six feet long was very expensive to produce. Normal furniture cane covered with headlining cloth was deemed to be an acceptable and cost effective replacement. Further changes to the interior included the moving of the rear passenger ashtrays from the rear of the front seat backrests to the rear seat armrest panels.

The design of the windscreen surround changed from the early rubber type with a central chrome strip, to a neater chromium frame with a much narrower central strip. This modification greatly improved forward vision.

A good quality Carrington Merlin tool kit was fitted in a separate compartment built into the substantially thick boot lid (and it's a proud owner today who can display a complete set of these tools when showing the car to admirers).

The two large instrument dials (previously black with white numerals), now had a beige background with maroon numerals. At the same time, the early four spoked black plastic rimmed Brooklands steering wheel was changed to a brown and cream flecked pattern. The black dials and steering

This frontal impression shows a much flatter line to the tops of the front wings.

The frontal treatment on styling impression drophead should be noted, with its very large headlights but with flush fitting sidelights. This design was designated AC 1946.

What might have been ... Was this an alternative production shape for the saloon, or a later styling change proposal? The following impressions show the car to be very Lancia like. The passenger cabin and frontal treatment is very clean, but the rear needs a little attention to create a more harmonious look.

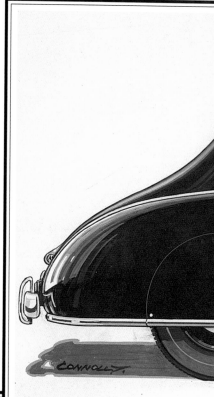

wheel looked far more sporty, but the factory standardised the change even though AC enthusiasts at the time complained about the new look dashboard. Perhaps the factory felt the car needed to look a little more conservative for mainstream buyers?

1948 saw the introduction of the Two-litre drophead coupé, one of which was featured in the 1952 film, *Folly to be Wise*. This particular car had several louvres along each side of the bonnet.

Later in 1948, the AC Buckland was produced, an open four/five-seater with a well fitted hood. The doors of the first cars, referred to as the Mark I, were given a straight line finish. This was soon changed, however, and the Mark II version had the more usual door cutaway. These cars were built at the Buckland works near Royston in Hertfordshire, with the running chassis supplied by AC.

Throughout production up to the

end of 1949 all cars were fitted with 17 inch rim wheels and tyres, with the exception of some Bucklands and dropheads which appear to have been fitted with 16 inch wheels and tyres. Incidentally, one 1949 car wore an unusual central drop - *a la* Jaguar - front bumper.

AC had produced nearly 500 cars by the end of 1949, and it was in this year that the AC Owners Club was formed. Over the coming years, with the added enthusiasm the Club brought to the marque, many Two-litres were campaigned on racing tracks around the country.

This 1948 AC demonstrator shows an unusual curved bumper treatment al la Jaguar. It's not clear whether this bumper was fitted at the factory.

Three quarter rear view in which the split rear window shape is not quite right. However, the Riley Pathfinder, which appeared many years later than this AC drawing, has a very similar waistline.

Neat headlight and front wing line with Ford influenced grill treatment? Again, very little work is needed to harmonise the pleasing lines of this design.

A 1946 mock-up model of what could have been. It looks very sleek compared to the production saloon and very like the Jaguar XK120 range. This surely would have been a winner for AC Cars, but perhaps it had too little headroom for the rear seat occupants if sold as a four-seater family car?

This rather poor picture shows the experimental car (L600) in very bad condition. It did its job, however, proving that the new radiator and lower positioned water pump were a success, as were the longer suspension springs.

The prototype Two-litre showing the rubber screen surround, also the bonnet emblem which, when pulled, opened the rear hinged bonnet.

Another view of the prototype Two-litre: the quick release rear wheel spats that were quickly discontinued.

In 1947 the car was regarded as having very clean lines.

This left hand drive car doesn't have the hood rail and is fitted with the neater chromed screen frame. The overall styling of the car is very attractive.

Perhaps the first drophead coupé, showing the solid rubber screen surround and central chrome strip. Only a couple of cars were built with the fixed rail over the door.

In the late 1940s this was the view most motorists saw of the Two-litre. This picture shows the additional bumper overiders which were an option from the factory.

Chassis, engine and gearbox details prior to body fitment.

Thirty cars and frames in various stages of assembly and completion, as production moved into full swing in 1949. (Courtesy AC Owners Club)

A line of new Two-litres and a Buckland ready for delivery or collection. (Courtesy of AC Owners Club).

The slow and complicated job of producing and assembling the ash body frame. (Courtesy of AC Owners Club)

An early AC Cars catalogue drawing depicting the new drophead coupé for 1947.

The Drophead Coupé

FOR those who enjoy the exhilaration of open car motoring but also at times desire the amenities of a closed car—this body has been designed.

The change-over from closed to open and vice versa is simple and quickly managed. When down, the hood folds away in the neatest manner.

The accommodation is identical with the Saloon and ease of entry and exit for the rear passengers is just as free, with no inconvenience for those in front.

A.C.'s have specialised for many years in building drop-head bodies and all their valuable experience is embodied in this model. Built in the A.C. tradition in our own Works.

CHARACTER

IN DESIGN • IN PERFORMANCE

TWO **AC** LITRE

MANY OUTSTANDING FEATURES • EXCEPTIONAL VISIBILITY

LOW GRAVITY CENTRE ENSURES AMAZING ROAD HOLDING

LIGHT ALUMINIUM BODY • 85 M.P.H. • 24 M.P.G.

A. C. CARS LIMITED

THAMES DITTON, SURREY

STAND
131
MOTOR SHOW EARLS COURT
LONDON OCT. 27—NOV. 6

Another catalogue drawing for 1949. It's interesting to note that not one car was built to this style with large headlights etc., and by 1949 the rear spats had also been discontinued.

The neat design and treatment to the front of the saloon changed very little throughout its production. The sidelights were later made to fit flush to the wing.

The aesthetically pleasing door step plate is a feature of the AC, executed on chromed brass with indented lettering. Later cars were fitted with anodised aluminium plates, presumably to cut ever-mounting production costs.

Another one off? A 1949 Two-litre with a one-piece flat dash sporting a variety of coloured instruments.

Six-cylinders, triple-carbs and plenty of polished engine surfaces make the AC engine look very purposeful. This shot also shows the thermostatically controlled electric choke nestling between carbs two and three, and the thermostatic switch situated in front of carb number one, which controls the choke.

Two photos of an AC bodied shooting brake built in the 'Woody' style on an Alvis chassis. The top picture shows the car in use with the Fairey Aviation Company. The second shows the condition the car was found in when discovered in a lock-up garage in the British midlands. Some unusual features of the body are the use of oak timber instead of ash for the framing, and the fact that only the equivalent of a bootlid opens at the rear, thus qualifying the car as a saloon rather than an estate. It also has two doors on the nearside and only one on the offside.

After the war cars were a scarce commodity. Farmers and tradesmen needed a vehicle that was practical and versatile for both passenger use and for carrying goods. Hence these strange looking estates and Woodies. Good looks were not the order of the day. Being long and wide the AC Two-litre chassis was perfect for these semi-utility vehicles and several were built.

Both of the cars shown on this page were built by Bamber and Co. in Southport in 1948. Very little is known about these cars and illustrations are rare, hence the use of these poor quality pictures.

The swivel quarterlight glass and knurled twisting knob can clearly be seen in this picture. Most cars were fitted with frameless quarter light glass, unlike this example.

Bulkhead details were similar on most Two-litres with fuse/control box, wiper motor, horn relay, coil, electric fuel pump and filter plus starter solenoid fitted to the nearside.

Adjustment mechanism for shortening/lengthening the steering column. Later cars were fitted with an additional hump on the engine side of the bulkhead to allow for greater steering wheel height adjustment. This is carried out by loosening the nuts under the dash and the steering box, adjusting to the desired height and then retightening.

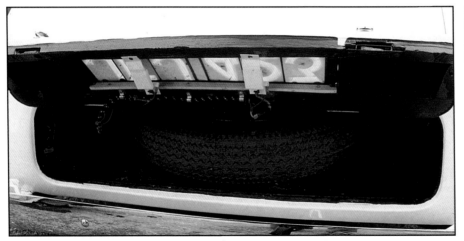

The spare wheel locker door showing the correct detailing and bulb holder fittings for illumination of the rear number plate.

An unusual sight on the Two-litre nowadays, a full set of Charrington Merlin tools.

The very large, heavy doors on the Two-litre were fitted with these novel wheels at their front edge to assist ease of closing. Wear normally takes place in the door hinges, the doors sag and these wheels get knocked off.

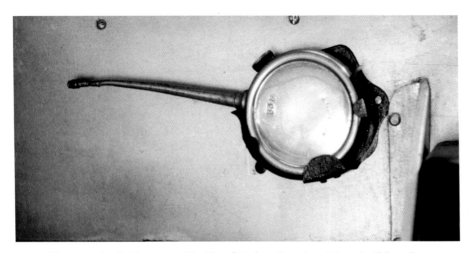

The practical oil can and holder fitted to the aluminium bulkhead.

5

PROGRESS THROUGH 1950 AND BEYOND

By the beginning of 1950, production of the Two-litre had settled down to approximately five cars per week. These production figures continued through 1950 and 1951.

There was growing competition in the motor industry, though, and by the end of 1951 the Two-litre was becoming very expensive. In September 1952, the basic price was £1214 plus British Purchase Tax of £675-18s-00d, making a total of £1889-18s-00d. Jaguar, Rover, Lea-Francis and Standard, for example, were producing cars equal to, if not better than, the AC Two-litre. Total production in 1952/1953 was down to 204 cars.

Steady improvements were still being made: four-wheel hydraulic brakes were now fitted, for example, and Woodhead Monroe hydraulic dampers were fitted to both axles. 16 inch wheels were now standard, and scuttle vents improved ventilation to front seat occupants. However, one motor magazine which tested the Two-litre commented that one of the biggest drawbacks of the car was the large

Finished in "National Grey" (a poor description of light green) this car was pictured in an AC sales brochure.

Year	Make & model	Price (inc. Purchase Tax)
1952	AC Saloon	£1889
1952	Jaguar MK VII Saloon	£1774
1952	Armstrong Siddeley Whitely Saloon	£1728
1952	Riley 2.5 Litre Saloon	£1642
1952	Rover 75 Saloon	£1487
1952	Wolseley Six Eighty	£1121

How the price of an AC Saloon compared with other models in 1952.

This X-ray side elevation clearly shows the layout of the engine and drivetrain, passenger compartment, fuel tank and luggage areas.

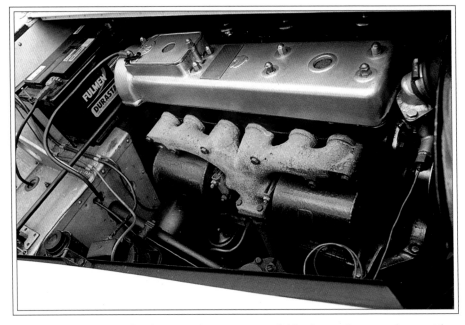

Offside engine details showing the extra manifold silencer boxes, along with the dynamo driven from a cross-shaft and, to the far left, the brake fluid reservoir.

amount of warm air being drawn into it, possibly through these vents.

The rear quarter light windows could now be opened, being hinged at their front edge, so as to improve ventilation for back seat occupants. The door quarterlight surround changed to a chromed brass section, which made opening and closing of the window easier and quicker.

The company's policy of producing only a single model had also changed, and the customer was now given a far greater choice. All models were still built on the standard chassis, but various body styles were listed: two-door saloon; Buckland sports; drophead coupé; four-door saloon; or two-door convertible (Coupé de Ville effect), and dual colour paintwork and interiors could also be ordered. Even with all of these options sales still slowed ...

With the introduction of the AC Ace open sports car and the Aceca closed coupe, though, AC was on to a couple of winners. Thirty-five Two-litre cars were built over 1954/1955, and between 1956 and 1958 the Two-litres were only made to special order, the last car leaving the works in May 1958. Some chassis were sent to specialist coachbuilders but little is known of them. At least two cars were built as estate cars, though no records exist to identify the coachbuilders: one looked very like a Woody estate, but both looked very strange indeed compared to the normal styling of the Two-litre saloon.

Engine brake horsepower (bhp) increased with the development of the

Ace sports car, with power for the Two-litre with CL engine specification up to 90bhp at 4500rpm (1957 figures*), on a compression ratio of 8:1.

The very last few Two-litres were very good cars indeed, beautifully built as always, of course, but by the late 'fifties they looked and felt very vintage.

* Various performance figures were quoted in road tests indicating acceleration of:
0 to 50mph in 14.6/16.0 seconds
0 to 60mph in 19.9/21.0 seconds
and a top speed of 80/85mph.

The full flow oil filter, which was fitted to later models of the Two-litre. Being positioned so close to the exhaust manifold doesn't help in trying to cool the oil.

Very few Two-litres were painted in the colour depicted in the sales brochure ("Beige Fonce" in this case). This 1951 example was owned by the author in the 1980s.

A very late 1954 car still showing the basic dash layout but fitted with dual coloured interior: ivory and blue with blue head cloth.

A lovely picture of the archetypal 1951 Two-litre with green paintwork.

Two Two-litres, both registered in March 1952, showing the variations in specification, such as roof mounted aerial, spotlights and overriders. The car on the right has the neat later style sidelights incorporating amber flashing indicator lights.

The standard dashboard layout. The lower car features the beige dials and the under-dash shelf and optional screen heater vents. The black switches for the spots should, the author thinks, be beige, like the rest of the switchgear.

A rare photo indeed. A brand new Two-litre, registered January 1, 1952 and with delivery mileage only, sitting on its new driveway and sporting a very pleasing maroon paint finish and extra chromed wheel embellishers.

Apart from some very early cars these chrome hubcaps with AC motif were standard for the entire production of the Two-litre and its variants.

Early cars had a pointed edge at the rear of the rear quarterlight. Later cars had the more curved finish as in this picture. The position of the trafficators can be clearly seen.

The rear quarterlight window and its opening mechanism can be clearly seen in this picture. This additional ventilation was very welcome for rear seat passengers.

Door quarterlight detail as found on later cars showing chromed brass frame and the simple lock handle instead of a rotating knurled wheel on the inside panel.

One of the most inviting interiors you could ask for. Giving armchair comfort, the Two-litre interior was always renowned for the quality of its leather and timber finish.

Opening scuttle vents were fitted in 1951 to improve the amount of cool air that could be directed to the footwells; no doubt they also helped water ingress to rot the ash timber doorframes ...

The AC drophead coupé looking very elegant with the hood down. The hood never folded completely flat on these cars.

The drophead showing off its pleasing lines with the hood up.

A hood cover was supplied which makes things more comfortable for rear seat occupants.

Rearward vision with the hood up was obviously not considered a priority in the drophead coupé's design.

The view for the rear seat passengers.

The very purposeful stance of the drophead.

6

THE BUCKLAND

Introduced in 1949, the Buckland Sports gave AC customers the option of having an open car. Approximately sixty cars were built by Ernie Bailey, friend of the Hurlock family and owner of the Buckland Body Works in Hertfordshire.

Ernie Bailey, and his idea for the Buckland, was just the tonic for AC Cars. Ernie was an entrepreneur who worked a very large farm in Buckland, just outside of Royston in Hertfordshire. Ernie was a generous and hard-working man, and his farmland was full of a variety of vegetables. He was very proud of his achievements and one of his favourite sayings was, "I employ half of the people in Buckland, and I feed the other half."

People were very poor after the war and Ernie turned a blind eye to people attempting to take small amounts of vegetables from his fields to feed their families. The farm produce was sent to Covent Garden where Ernie's brother, Bill Bailey, looked after wholesaling and distribution from an office in Henrietta Street.

Ernie had an excellent singing voice and, in the early 1940s, was persuaded to take singing lessons at the Royal College of Music. This led to an introduction to one of the College's piano teachers, Joan Lane. Her beauty swept Ernie off his feet and they were married in 1943.

With a flair for design and engineering, Ernie had the vision to build bodies on other car manufacturers' chassis, and a couple of experimental Bucklands were made by independent coachbuilders before production started at the Buckland works. Ernie gathered together a small workforce of craftsmen each with the individual skills that were required for his car body building project. Most of the workers were local to the Royston area, people like Harold Eden (manager), Sam Wightman (the foreman), Eric Campbell (cutting and shaping the ash timber), Archie Allen (a superb upholstery trimmer) and his assistant Ruby, Fred Miller and his son George (who did most of the fitting up), Stephan (an Italian prisoner of war who assembled the bodies), Keith Bullard (mechanic), Stan Coxall (general fitter), Mike Davin (maintenance), Peter Cole (metalwork and hood framing), Ron Clayton (paint preparation), and, of course, John Tojeiro of AC Ace fame (who carried out the paint spraying). It was actually Ernie Bailey who introduced John Tojeiro to the directors of AC Cars in 1953, so they could see John's idea for the ladder framed all independently sprung sports racing car. Ernie appointed Mrs Joan Clarke to keep the books and thus everything was ready to roll.

The first cars produced were Woody estates (shooting brakes), one on a Ford 10 chassis and the other on an ex-army Standard 14hp chassis. This car then had its windows covered to enable it to run (as a van) on red petrol, both cars being used as general works vehicles. With valuable experience gained from building these cars, the company purchased two chassis from Alvis (numbers 20662 and 20675) in late 1946.

Ernie Bailey's wife, Joan, pictured at the wheel of the new AC Buckland in this Buckland brochure picture.

The chassis were used to build further shooting brakes. Unfortunately, as records were not kept, it's not clear whether these cars were supplied by AC, or by Buckland Body Works.

By 1949, the AC Buckland was well into production and a brochure was produced with the glamorous Joan Bailey modelling as the driver of the car illustrated on the cover. This must have amused Ernie and Joan since she couldn't drive at the time and, unbeknown to all admirers of the brochure car, one of her baby daughters (Catherine) was on the back seat in a

carrycot! It should also be mentioned that Joan Bailey was used as the model for the AC Petite brochure, along with her daughter Angela, the Petite being produced in response to the oil crisis caused by the Suez war.

Ernie and Joan were game for anything and on several occasions trusted AC and Buckland cars on long Continental trips. On one such trip they tested the Petite to its limits by driving non-stop from Calais to Cannes to check its endurance.

To return to the Buckland, on early cars, the Mark I, for example, the

door line was straight. This soon changed, however, to the more familiar cutaway door style. The layout of the dash and instruments were also very different to the two-door saloon, the dash being placed deeper and lower than in the saloon, and the Buckland also boasted a rev counter. Several internal door styles were used: early cars, for example, had a variety of different ways of attaching the side screen in place, later Bucklands had wind up windows in the doors.

There were minor variations between the majority of cars, such as

57

BUCKLAND MARK I.

BUCKLAND MARK I.

BUCKLAND MARK II.

These pictures from the original brochure show the Mark I with the straight cut door treatment, also known as the Italian line, and the Mark II, with its cutaway door line. All Bucklands had a very good hood with various side screen systems.

An aerial shot of Buckland House and its farm outbuildings. All the upholstery work for the Buckland cars was completed in the long single storey building behind the house.

headlight position and front and rear wing design, and one car even boasted a completely different front end forward of the bulkhead. This car was actually examined in 1992 and, although in very poor condition, it was clear that the entire front panelling of the car (wings and radiator surround) was made in one piece, with a flat centrally hinged bonnet reminiscent of the Bristol 401. The only panel that appears to be interchangeable with normal Bucklands was the radiator cowl.

Another version of the Buckland received a rather *avant-garde* treatment to the rear wings, giving a very attractive scalloped finish.

In the early 1950s, the Buckland gave AC buyers the blend of family practicability and good sporting handling they desired. It still needed to shed weight, of course, and the engine could have done with more power. However, the AC management was slow to increase compression ratios, as the engine was still running with white metal big-end bearings, and reliability rather than power was the order of the day.

Ernie always enjoyed the razzmatazz of motor shows and he always put in his fair share of time on the AC stand. At one early 1950s motor show the comedian Norman Wisdom visited the AC stand and spent a great deal of time with Ernie mulling over the attributes of the Buckland. Ernie

explained and demonstrated how easy it was to fold and stow the hood. However, as luck would have it, the hood wasn't going to oblige on this occasion. Norman Wisdom grasped the opportunity to help and then proceeded to do his unfolding and setting up the deck chair routine using Ernie's Buckland hood as the prop. Of course Norman Wisdom got his feet and arms caught in the hood mechanism and generally caused mayhem on the stand with his shrieks and howls of laughter. He soon had a crowd around the AC stand, and Ernie along with everyone else was in fits of laughter.

When things had quietened down, Norman spent some more time chatting with Ernie and was so taken with his pleasant attitude and charm that he gave Ernie his personal telephone number so they could stay in touch.

As AC's chassis records are rather

An early fifties photo of the Buckland workers on a river Thames trip to Windsor along with some of the Bailey family's Covent Garden staff. From front of boat left to right: Row 1. The farm transport manager, Covent Garden staff, Ernie Bailey, Joan Bailey. Row 2. Mr and Mrs Lane (Joan Bailey's parents). Row 3. W. Williams, Mr and Mrs Bailey senior. Row 4. Ben Preston (mechanic), Stan Coxall (fitter), Eric Campbell (woodworker), unknown, unknown. Row 5. Mrs Woods, Mr Woods (accountant). Row 6. Unknown, unknown, Mr Pammeter (sprayer), Fred Miller senior (woodwork), Les Sell (farm worker), Diana Daniels (Secretary). Row 7. Ruby Brown (upholstery), Archie Allen (upholstery), Harold Eden (Manager), Mrs Valerie Eden. Row 8. Ron Clayton, unknown (apprentice), George Miller junior (woodworker), Hubert Strange (mechanic), George Hayden (mechanic). Row 9. All unknown.

Joan Bailey modelling alongside the AC Petite in Cannes after its successful test run from Calais.

vague, and no Buckland factory records seem to exist, it appears that production of the Buckland Sports ceased in 1953, although AC continued building a few of these cars itself at Thames Ditton.

In 1954-55, Ernie Bailey tried out another idea by using the AC Petite chassis and building an enclosed three-wheeler rickshaw-type vehicle. Although approximately twenty examples were built, it wasn't considered a success and production of all cars ceased at the Buckland works.

The start of it all for Buckland Body Works. Ernie Bailey with the first car built. This estate shooting brake was used as a general runabout for the farm and the body works.

One of the Alvis chassis shooting brakes built at Ernie Bailey's Buckland Body Works.

This picture, taken in London, shows the very first Buckland produced. It was built by an independent coachbuilder and it features Archie Allen at the wheel. Archie worked for Park Ward and he was asked by Ernie Bailey to carry out the trimming work on the first two cars. Ernie was so impressed with Archie's high quality workmanship, he asked him to move to the Royston area to become Buckland's full time trimmer. Archie duly agreed.

Ernie Bailey experimented with two-tone paintwork as this picture, taken in France, shows. The two–tone paintwork emphasises the car's very pleasing lines. It should be noted that this car carries the same registration number (LNK 289) as the special Buckland with the different headlight treatment (below). Did Ernie transfer the registration plate or replace the unusual front wings with standard items and repaint the car two-tone?

Viewed from this angle the different treatment to the front wing and the door panel line can be seen. The line has been taken to the bottom rear of the door. Later versions carried the line higher and further along the body to join the rear wing.

The Bailey family always enjoyed continental travel. This shot shows Ernie's wife Joan with Ernie's father Bill Bailey alongside his AC Saloon on the Cote d'Azure in the early 1950s.

The Buckland dash is uncluttered with three clear dials. The rev counter is on the left, the oil, water temperature, fuel and amp meter is in the centre, and the speedometer is on the right. A matching dial-sized cubbyhole is on the left of the dash. This picture also shows the neat fitting of the ashtray and window winder in the door panel, plus the door cubbyhole and the knurled fittings for the quarterlights.

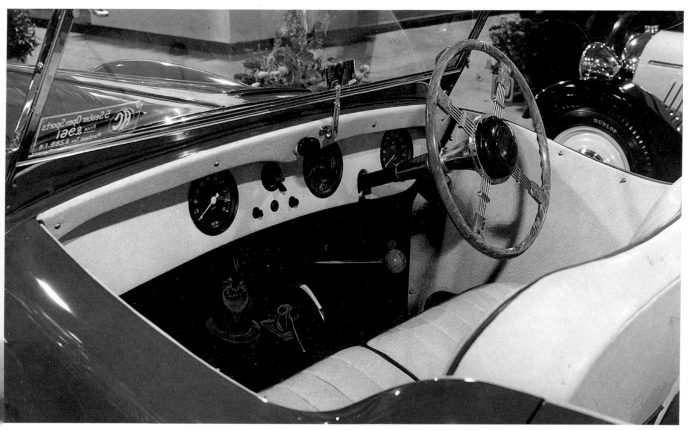

Two pictures of a Buckland taken at the Earls Court motor show. They show the flush-fitting side lights and the interior trim details of the 1950 model. The information on the screen indicates that the five-seater open sports model costs £961 plus purchase tax of £289.80.

Another version of the Buckland with a plain door finish, no wind up windows and no ashtrays. It was probably felt that, being an open top car, the world was your ashtray.

No doubt trying to get to grips with the three-wheeler motoring concept, this photo of Ernie Bailey was taken in Italy in 1952.

A 1950 Buckland resting in the Derbyshire countryside.

A 1951 Buckland in competition. This picture shows how well the car maintains its composure, with little roll when taking bends at high speed.

This is indeed a rare photo, on two counts. One, the very unusual position of the headlights, low down on the front wings, gives the car a very aggressive stance. Two, Ernie Bailey is driving and his brother Bill is the passenger. The photo was taken at the Concourse D'Elegance in Brighton and whatever the marshall on the left of the picture drank at lunchtime seems to be working. This Buckland was featured in the 1951 Alistair Sim film 'Laughter in Paradise'.

One of AC Cars' Scottish dealers, T.M. Gilroy displaying a Buckland at a Scottish motor show in 1950.

Ernie Bailey at the wheel of the Buckland with his lady colleague about to collect their prize at the Brighton Concourse D'Elegance.

Wind up windows and quarterlight fittings of a Buckland.

Quarterlight and rear channel guide in place to assist location of the perspex panel when being raised or lowered by the door winder.

By the end of 1951 the Buckland was developed to its best, with neat detailing and hood arrangement. This car has rather attractive, scalloped rear wings. Only two cars were given this rear wing style.

Most Bucklands differed from the Two-litre saloons in not having a door step/running board under the door.

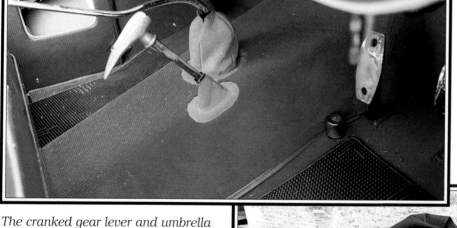

The cranked gear lever and umbrella type handbrake lever were fitted to all of the AC Two-litre range, as was the headlight dipping switch on the floor close to the gearbox.

The neat hood arrangement could be completely folded away under cover. Armchair comfort was the order of the day for the rear seat occupants in the Buckland.

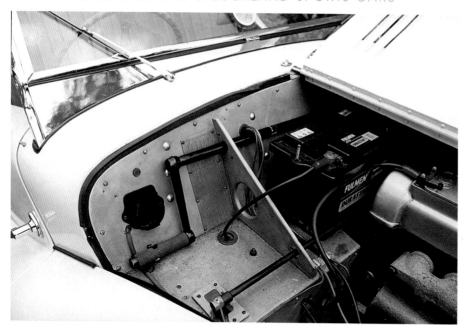

Offside bulkhead of the Buckland
with brass chassis number plate and
(empty) oil can holder. Fitting the
starting handle on the bulkhead is
unusual as it's normally fitted in the
boot.

A rare sight, two Bucklands side by side.

Frontal treatment of the 1951 Buckland, with flush fitting sidelights and extended arm wing mirrors.

This picture shows off the Buckland's lines at their best.

Ernie Bailey and his father Bill, with a Buckland and saloon keeping them company.

A left hand drive Buckland, looking splendid with white coachwork and contrasting red leather interior.

'Only Fools and Horses' beware, a special AC Petite being worked hard at the Buckland works. It's not clear if AC or Buckland built the body.

This picture, taken in California in 1952, shows a left hand drive Buckland with the two-tone paintwork much favoured by Ernie Bailey. It shows a third colour used on the wheel rims to match the interior trim. The non-standard very high overriders were probably an American bolt-on accessory.

7

FOUR-DOOR
AND
SPECIAL CARS

In 1951, AC produced one four-door version of the saloon. Although being more practical for family use, the car lost some of its sleekness as the front doors were reduced in length to accommodate rather small rear doors. The normal vertically-pleated leather-covered seats were changed on this model to a centrally-pleated cushion on all seats, with a plain leather surround. Although slow to catch on, by the beginning of 1953, the four-door became quite a popular alternative to the two-door. Approximately forty-seven four-door saloons were built between 1951 and 1957.

Another car that should be mentioned is the AC convertible. This car was built for the 1952 Motor Show and it appears to have been a one-off. Whether it was too expensive or just impractical to build more of them we don't know. This car did have some major differences to the normal drophead. The single petrol tank, for example, which was normally fitted between the rear passengers and the boot, was moved and separate petrol tanks were fitted under each front wing, the filler caps being positioned at the rear of each wing. With the petrol tank now gone from behind the boot, AC was able to make the boot deeper. Access to the boot and spare wheel was made easier by changing the normal practice of having separate boot lid and spare wheel locker doors into one large boot lid and spare wheel cover which was hinged at its top edge. However, for all of the work in this area, very little extra space was generated.

The convertible looked very smart,

the rear windows wound down into the bodywork and, with the hood folded, the car had very pleasing lines. The trafficators were moved to the rear of the front wings, and the normal raised panel line running along the length of the car from the scuttle to the rear wing was omitted.

This car proved that Thames Ditton still retained its coachbuilding craftsmen. To build a one-off car like this, with all the intricacies involved in making the glass frame and getting a mechanism to make the rear windows fold away into the basic saloon body to work must have taken much head scratching.

Another car of interest was the last Two-litre produced. This was registered in May 1958, registration number HDJ 286. The photos show a change to the rear lights, from the usual round flush-fitting type to a more modern angled MGA type glass. Close inspection of the dashboard reveals one large speedo dial, along with four smaller dials, possibly taken from the AC Ace dashboard stores. A round heater can be seen peeping from below the dash with various other switches on the dash in front of the driver. At this time the factory had developed the engine to its best specification yet, and contemporary comments stated that the AC engine ran with turbine smoothness, no doubt helped by the new torsional vibration-damping wheel fitted to the front of the crankshaft. It's strange to think that this car was still fitted with pop-up directional trafficators!

AC always prided itself on the

A.C. CARS LTD. THAMES DITTON, SURREY.

THE NEW FOUR DOOR SALOON

Hand tailored throughout, the coachwork represents the finest practice in British craftsmanship. Quality leather on Dunlopillo cushioning provides exceptional comfort. Body and wings entirely panelled in aluminium gives lightness and freedom from rust. The styling retains the reputation for perfect fore and aft vision to driver and passengers. Mounted on the well known two-litre chassis a perfect combination is achieved, when flexibility for town, and high speed touring in the country, is required.

The AC four-door sales brochure print for 1953.

quality finish of its cars and this was also reflected in the owner's handbook. It's interesting to note that even though a description of each item on the dashboard was given, the handbook didn't show a photo or drawing of the dashboard. However, it did explain in depth how to strip the engine, gearbox and back axle!

At this point another interesting car that should be mentioned is a four door saloon fitted with wire wheels. This appears to have been the only car given this treatment. The effect is not very good, though, and one wonders if the wheels would have been more appropriate on the Buckland, or other open versions of the AC?

The leather seats on the four-door were stitched using a different style of pleating. A small armrest on the rear door is just visible here.

This side view of a four-door car in need of a respray shows the central pillar to which front and rear doors are hinged, also the changed detail to the frame of the front quarterlight using metal instead of wood.

FIVE SEATER CONVERTIBLE

The A.C. range of coachwork on the two-litre chassis has now been extended to include the above Convertible. Wide doors ensure easy entrance and exit. Careful design allows beauty of line to be allied to snug protection. With the hood down and neatly stowed, the full benefit of open car motoring can be enjoyed, and yet with the hood up and the close fitting glass windows raised, the protection of closed car motoring is amply ensured. The forward portion of the hood folds back to provide Coupe de Ville effect, and the large quarter lights and rear view window allows uninterrupted vision to side and rear both to the driver and passengers alike. Two 6-gallon petrol tanks mounted on either side of scuttle under rear of front wings allows rear luggage locker to be increased to 10 cu. ft.

Sales brochure for the convertible.

The 1952/53 Motor Show drophead coupé in its original light green paintwork.

This picture shows the petrol filler cap positioned on the rear of the front wing. Pop-up indicators were still being fitted to the AC, and on this car they were fitted at the very rear of the front wings. With the hood down the car had clean pleasing lines. The raised panel flash usually seen on the door and rear panels was omitted.

Rear window fully raised on the Coupé De Ville/Convertible. The neat hood detail can also be seen here.

The neat execution of window winder and interior light fittings in the convertible.

The simple treatment of the one-piece bootlid/spare wheel compartment lid, which gives the rear of the car a very uncluttered look.

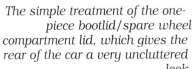

Only one car was fitted with wire wheels, a 1955 four-door. The red wheels look rather strange, perhaps if finished in grey or silver they would look more pleasing?

Different instrument layout for the last Two-litre Saloon, now sporting the smaller Ace-type individual dials, with the original speedo in beige (since changed to black), but still no rev counter. (Courtesy of AC Owners Club)

8

RACING AND RALLYING THE TWO-LITRE

Up to the early 'fifties, AC Cars had never promoted the Two-litre for motor racing. This was mostly left to enthusiastic owners. The factory did enter the works demonstrator in various rallying events, but without any great success. The car was normally driven by Derek Hurlock. Although really too big for trials and rallying, the Two-litre performed very well on the smooth tarmac found on the race circuits dotted around the country. The most famous drive was by Jim Mayers at Silverstone in the Production Touring Car Race on May 10th 1952. The car's speed and handling on corners created quite a stir, with one onlooker commenting; "I didn't know the postwar AC could motor so fast," and another, remarking on independently-suspension cars, "How pleasant it is to see front wheels stand up straight on corners," as the Two-litre AC swept past a Bristol. Others at the meeting were also full of enthusiasm and praise. The editor of *Autosport* magazine quoted the following: "Moss and Wharton were both lapping around 2 mins 19 seconds, whilst Jim Mayers was giving an extraordinary display in an AC saloon with over 40,000 miles on the clock. Mayers was actually leading the entire Bristol contingent with the exception of Tony Crook."

The AC finished ninth out of fifteen and came second to Crook in the over one and a half and under two litre class.

Club racing was very popular in the early 'fifties and, as photos show, there were plenty of owners and drivers prepared to put the cars on race circuits

A pre-1950 saloon looking very clean at a checkpoint in the 1955 Bournemouth Rally. Entrant R.A.B. McFie.

Entrant 342 taking part in the 1953 Daily Express Rally. (Courtesy of Ferret Fotographics)

Jim Mayers, whose famous drive in a Two-litre caused such a stir at Silverstone, here showing his skill at the wheel of a Lester MG in 1952. (Courtesy of Ferret Fotographics)

A Buckland holding the inside line against an Alvis on the smooth Silverstone surface. (Courtesy National Motor Museum, Beaulieu)

The Two-litre in Felixstowe showing its steadiness when cornered hard, whilst competing in the 1953 Coronation Rally. (Courtesy National Motor Museum, Beaulieu)

Driver J. Williamson participating in the MCC National Rally in 1952. (Courtesy National Motor Museum, Beaulieu)

Entrant number 290's navigator either at a checkpoint or needing a smoke break on the 1952 London Rally. Note the unusual foglamp position. (Courtesy National Motor Museum, Beaulieu)

MPL 340 being campaigned in the 1952 RAC Rally.

A lovely 1953 shot of various Two-litre ACs in the paddock at Silverstone, getting ready to do battle in the AC race. At least 12 ACs can be seen in this photo. (Courtesy of AC Owners Club)

and drive them to their limits.

A saloon was entered in the 1949 Monte Carlo Rally. However, a mistake was made at an overseas filling station. It appears that the car was filled with diesel and the time lost in cleaning out the petrol tank was too great to achieve a good overall time. Another attempt was made in 1951, but map reading errors led to another poor result.

Overall, the Buckland appeared to be the best version of the Two-litre for motor racing. It was lighter than the saloon and, with the screen removed and a tonneau cover fitted, was probably the more aerodynamically efficient car.

Top - Driver Lass in the Two-litre Saloon leads a group of ACs driven by Wilkinson, Nightingale, Hurlock, Day and Ridge in a club race in the early 1950s. Centre & above - Various Two-litres, Bucklands and pre-war ACs in the same race. (Courtesy AC Owners Club)

Two rather fuzzy shots of the June 4th 1955 8's Club meeting, showing a variety of pre- and postwar ACs with Two-litre Saloons and a Buckland drophead in the middle of the grid. (Courtesy of AC Owners Club)

A group of Two-litre cars about to set off on a point to point rally on a very cold day in 1956. The picture clearly shows the straight door treatment on the early Bucklands. (Courtesy of AC Owners Club)

The factory car, driven at Redhill by Derek Hurlock, shifting plenty of gravel on its way to fourth place in a driving test rally in 1952. AC experimented with this car and it was even fitted with independent front suspension, but the results were not considered successful enough to change the existing beam axle arrangement for production cars.

A lovely study of the handling characteristics of the Buckland at speed on the smooth Silverstone track in 1953. The car sits very square and shows virtually no roll. With screen folded flat and several trim items removed, the car may have been able to top 100mph. OUR 67 was Ernie Bailey's personal car loaned for the day.

A Buckland streamlined as much as possible. No large flat screen or number plate just a small aero screen and tonneau cover. Driver H.F. Day at the wheel at the 8's Club meeting, Silverstone 1952. (Courtesy of AC Owners Club)

9

TUNING THE TWO-LITRE ENGINE

INTRODUCTION

The AC Two-litre engine benefited greatly from steady development throughout its production life, eventually producing approximately 105-110bhp in the early 1960s. This was with a nitrided hardened crankshaft, shell bearing bottom end and running a compression ratio of 9:1.

The following information is a guide to the various options available to those owners who want a little bit extra from their car. Good increases in power can be achieved without sacrificing reliability or economy, but the author cannot stress enough that if power improvements are to be made, it's absolutely essential that the bottom end (mains and big ends) are in first class condition. It's pointless fitting high compression pistons or skimming the cylinder head without first attending to the bottom end because, otherwise, the big end bearings will simply fail within a few hundred miles.

It's also important to point out that the methods described here should be considered as general guidelines, not specific recommendations. This is because, over the years, work may already have been carried out on the engine and it's impossible to recommend specific modifications without first knowing what has been done already.

The first step in tuning the AC engine is to ensure that careful measurements and calculations are made by qualified personnel so as to ensure that all adjustments are within tolerance.

CRANKSHAFT, FLYWHEEL AND DAMPERS

The crankshaft runs in five main bearings, with the rear bearing situated at the flywheel being larger than the rest. The crankshaft is actually stronger than its spindly looks might suggest though one motor engineer once commented to me, "That looks more like a bent coat-hanger than a crankshaft!" Grinding of the main bearings and big ends should be kept to a minimum, and the journals should not be ground more than 0.030in from standard if it can be helped. It's essential that all journal and bearing recess machining work be carried out to the highest standards and within close tolerances.

The rear of the crankshaft carries a bronze skew gear which drives the cross-shaft for the dynamo, the distributor, and the oil pump. It's very important to check that, when carrying out line boring of main bearings, it's kept as central as possible: if this is not monitored the bronze skew gear can mesh too heavily with the cross-shaft gear.

Detailed specifications and dimensions of the crankshaft and engine are given in the *AC Saloon Owners' Manual* which is readily available from the AC Owners Club.

Up until the late 'fifties, most AC Two litre engines leaked oil from the back of the crank onto the face of the flywheel. It's very worthwhile, therefore, to obtain a modern seal to fit into the block and sump. Some machining will be required, but this is the time to do it, with the block stripped and the

Baffle plates in place in the sump (oil pan) clearly showing how the oil is now trapped in the pick up area under harsh braking and fast right hand bends. Note the extra hole drilled into the anti-surge plate for the dipstick to fit through.

sump temporarily refitted to facilitate accurate machining. It should be noted that sumps and blocks were originally matched for machining, so if a different sump is fitted, critical seal dimensions might vary. During rebuild it's also wise to fit the front oil seal when the sump has been loosely fitted to the block. The front seal can then be gently tapped into place and the sump nuts tightened.

Postwar engines up to UMB 1798 were fitted with a very substantial and heavy split flywheel. The flywheel components were bolted together using six rubber mountings placed between the two flywheel surfaces. This arrangement acts as a torsional damper to eliminate most vibrations which would otherwise be transmitted from the crankshaft. Flywheels fitted after UMB 1798 were solid, however, with a torsional damper unit fitted to the front of the crankshaft instead. If you are using a split flywheel it's important to check the quality of the damper rubbers and fit new ones if needed. The later engine, with its solid flywheel and front damper, is generally agreed to be a better option. Having said that, a later engine with a damper in poor condition will vibrate more than a well assembled split flywheel with good damper rubbers.

One of the main problems with the front damper is that the rubber jointing material begins to split, thus creating an out of balance force at high revolutions. One possible solution it is to carefully pour a liquid rubber solution into any cracks and allow this to set. This remedy has worked on

several occasions, but should be regarded as a short term fix. The only other and better solution, of course, is to fit a new damper.

OIL PUMP AND OIL DISTRIBUTION
The oil pump is situated at the bottom

of the sump (oil pan), near the rear. The pump on early postwar engines had small straight-cut gears, and is quite a serviceable unit. This was soon upgraded, however, to a helical gear unit, which gave a much-improved performance. The latter type are

The baffle plate around the oil pump housing and the position of the pick up pipe in the sump.

available through the Club spares section.

Oil pressure should not be over 80psi. In the author's experience, it's best to set the relief valve at 70psi, which should be produced at 2500rpm. The pressure will drop to approximately 15-20psi at tickover.

Oil pressure in the AC engine can drop alarmingly when there is wear in the oil pump body, and the engine tends to run a rather high oil temperature too (which thins the oil and reduces pressure). A very simple and economical modification is to fit a good quality oil cooler in front of the radiator. This will keep the oil temperature much lower and the oil pressure gauge needle at a much higher reading, adding protection to the engine. In many cases, fitting an oil

cooler will obviate the need to replace a slightly worn oil pump.

Oil surge is a common problem with the AC engine too, and there will be a loss of pressure on long right hand bends and when braking sharply. This is because the oil pump is situated on the right of the sump, near the rear. To overcome this surging and consequent pump starvation you need to build a copper baffle plate over the entrance to the oil pump. Brazed to this baffle plate is a 19mm diameter copper pipe, bent so that its base is 5mm from the base of the sump (in order to avoid picking up loose particles from the bottom), and finishing in the region of 50mm from the step-up in the sump. The second step is the fitting of a simple 90° baffle plate which is attached to the shelf section of the sump and extends

towards the rear of the sump for approximately 100mm. This traps oil and stops it rushing to the front of the engine. With these two simple additions (see photograph) oil surge should be virtually eliminated. All fixing bolts should be treated with a suitable sealing compound and fibre/copper washers should be used to ensure no oil leaks through bolthole fixings.

CONRODS AND BIG ENDS
Conrods and their big ends play a vital part in allowing the AC engine to achieve high revs and to use a higher compression ratio. The AC conrods are very long and thin and it's very important that they and their small and big ends are in perfect condition to allow for higher loads created by higher revs and increased compression. Small

nd bearings should be renewed as a matter of course.

The postwar engine originally had a compression ratio of 6.5:1. Pistons which raised the ratio to 7.5:1 became available later. The original conrod big ends had cast on white metal bearings which are reliable for all normal driving up to 4500rpm, for example). However, if CR ratios of 8:1 and over are employed, together with higher revs, the author's advice is to fit shell-type big end bearings. Austin Healey Sprite shells are quite suitable, and your local machine shop can advise on machining the conrods to accept them. The crankshaft journals have to be ground down for these bearings to fit, but the author never suffered a broken crank when racing with this modification.

It will be noted that a single shell is much narrower than the standard white metal bearing surface, and the most satisfactory job is to fit two shells alongside each other in the bearing journal. It should also be noted that the shell bearings will sit proud of the sides of the conrod when the bearing cap is replaced. Both face sides of the shells will need to be machined to reduce the width to the required crankshaft bearing, allowing for correct conrod endfloat of 0.0015in. If single shells only are fitted, it's essential that the sides of the conrods need to be metal sprayed and then machined (where the white metal used to sit on the outside edge), so as to give correct conrod endfloat of 0.0015in. Each conrod and cap will have to be machined to accept the raised locating nib of

each shell bearing: this is essential.

Although this change to shell bearings requires time and patience, the finished job is worth the effort as the engine can then rev safely and reliably to over 5000rpm with no ill effects (unless the crankshaft has a flaw). However, no engine with these modifications should be run without its major rotating and reciprocating parts being balanced professionally to very fine tolerances. With the foregoing modifications it will usually be possible to rev the engine to 5500rpm, but only for very short periods unless a new steel crank and racing conrod rods are fitted.

PISTONS/COMPRESSION RATIOS AND LINERS

Piston crown heights and, therefore, compression ratios can vary and today's selection of high quality pistons gives the engine tuner a wide choice. Piston compression ratios can be determined using the following rough guide. All measurements are taken from the centre of the gudgeon pin to the top surface of the piston:

    36mm = 6.5:1 ratio
    37.5mm = 7.0:1 ratio
    38.75mm = 8.0:1 ratio
    40.00mm = 9.0:1 ratio
    41.00mm = 10.0:1 ratio

Accordingly, if 8.0:1 pistons have been fitted, and 1.25mm is removed from the surface of the head, the compression ratio will be increased to 9.1.

At the end of its production life in

1963, the AC engine was running with a compression ratio of 9.0:1, and this figure is quite acceptable today. Of course, lower ratios can be used if deemed appropriate. For the purposes of this chapter, however, we are trying to gain extra power with good reliability through higher compression ratios and higher revs.

It should be remembered that the more you rev the engine the more power it produces. A compression ratio of 10.5:1 can be run quite satisfactorily providing the conrod bearing and oil system modifications previously mentioned have been carried out. Although higher ratios can be used, bearing reliability will suffer at high revs, and low octane fuel will cause pinking/knocking.

The cylinder liners work very well, and the installation instructions in the AC manual are quite satisfactory. For racing, it's quite acceptable to overbore the liners by 0.040in from standard, though it's essential to have the correct sized pistons beforehand.

When selecting pistons, the size you choose will, of course, depend on whether the liners are standard or have been rebored. The maximum oversize boring that can be used is 0.040in, which will also give a slightly greater cubic capacity. Various compression ratio pistons are available and it's important to check the measurement from the centre of the gudgeon pin to the top of the piston surface to ascertain the compression ratio of the existing pistons or the new ones that are going to be fitted.

If a higher compression ratio is

All distributor parts need to be disassembled, cleaned and put safely to one side. Careful note should be taken of how the advance/retard mechanism works, for reassembly.

required, but the existing pistons are to be retained, it can be achieved satisfactorily by having the cylinder head surface skimmed. This procedure gives two benefits: the compression ratio will be raised and the gasket face of the head will be trued. It will be noted that the cylinder head face has six circular rings cut into it so as to create a raised ring on the gasket surface. However, I have found no detriment to the sealing of the combustion gases by removal of this groove, provided that the liners have been well fitted and that all of the liner shoulders are sitting at the same height above the cylinder block. The groove on the head can be completely removed, though care must be taken not to remove so much metal as to allow the sparkplugs to protrude into the combustion chamber and foul the top of the piston liners when the head is tightened down.

It's wise to be cautious when fitting higher compression pistons because, if the head has already been skimmed, serious damage could occur by raising the compression ratio beyond what you first thought was correct.

IGNITION TIMING
The standard static ignition timing of 20° BTDC is a good starting point for setting the timing. However, with higher compression ratios it's useful to set the advance/retard at its mid point, and then start the engine and warm it thoroughly. Set the revs to approximately 2000rpm, slacken the pinch bolt holding the distributor and turn the body anti-clockwise to advance

the ignition timing. It will be noted that the engine will begin to run very smoothly at first, becoming rougher the more advance it's given. Turn the distributor until the engine is running at its smoothest, and, just before being advanced too much, tighten the pinch bolt. It's important to run the engine at 2000rpm, as the automatic advance weights in the distributor base will have moved and the true optimum advance setting can be ascertained. It's always wise when tuning the engine to fit new distributor bob weight springs, Lucas part number 407256/S.

MAJOR IGNITION ADJUSTMENTS AND TIMING
Up until now we have looked at adjusting the ignition timing without any reworking of the distributor. It

must be remembered that, as you increase the compression ratio, from say 7:1 to 8:1 or 9:1, the static ignition timing will need to be retarded to enable the starter motor to turn the engine over. Remember, the higher the compression the more the ignition needs to be retarded.

In normal tune the Two-litre ignition timing is set at 20° BTDC static. The automatic advance mechanism and springs give a further 15°, or so, of advance, giving a total of 35° advance, with maximum advance being reached at 1400-1500rpm.

If the engine has had the compression ratio raised to 8:1 or 9:1 the static timing will need to be reduced to 10° BTDC. Therefore, with the standard automatic advance mechanism only 25° total advance will be achieved, which, for a highly tuned

This picture, taken from below the baseplate, clearly shows the modified (previously circular) holes with the snail shell shape that should be achieved so the weight registers can move in an arc. The cam-like filed self taping screw can be seen on the left to act as an adjuster if the bob weights are moving out (advancing) too far.

This picture shows the springs installed and in tension, i.e. just pulling the bob weights apart.

engine, will be totally unsatisfactory.

In the following paragraphs we will go through the procedure of reworking the springs and baseplate in the distributor to enable the advance mechanism to give a much wider range of advance through the rev range.

The final ignition timing we are trying to achieve is a static timing of 10° BTDC with the automatic advance mechanism adjusting the timing as follows:

1000rpm	15° BTDC
1500rpm	20° BTDC
2000rpm	25° BTDC
2500rpm	30° BTDC
3000rpm	35° BTDC
3500rpm	42° BTDC

The absolute maximum total advance the timing should be set at is 44° BTDC at 3500rpm. Any more than this will make the engine run very roughly and will hammer the big ends. With the above settings the engine will run very smoothly, and spitting back through the carburettors should not be encountered.

No two AC engines are the same, of course, but the above figures are good guidelines to work to. If it is found that the engine is running too roughly, for example, the overall maximum advance can be reduced by a couple of degrees (thus each area in the rev range from 0 to 5000rpm will have its advance reduced). However, it's only the maximum advance at 3500 revs that should be reduced by adjustment of the baseplate.

The highest possible octane petrol should always be used. If pinking does occur, however, a high octane booster additive should be used rather than retarding the ignition. With the rev range settings already described pinking shouldn't be a problem.

The first job when modifying the distributor is to strip it down and replace any worn parts, such as the spindle bearing. Wear in the spindle will show up at higher revs and cause the points to open wider the higher up the rev range the engine is taken, thus changing the auto advance mechanism timing we are trying to achieve.

With the distributor stripped down and all parts cleaned, work can commence on the baseplate. The accompanying picture shows the two holes in which the bob weights register. The outside edge of the holes need to be filed to allow the weights to move out further, thus allowing greater automatic advance. The locating pins on the underneath of the weights move in an arc, NOT in a straight line, and care should be taken to remove metal from the correct area on the side of the hole. Again, the picture shows the approximate arc travel of the locating pin of the weight. The final dimension across the hole should be in the region of 14mm. The end results will only be known when the engine is run, of course, and small adjustments to the amount of metal removed from the edges of the holes may be required.

If it's found that you have removed too much metal from the hole edges, and that the engine is over advancing at 3500rpm, a simple solution is to fit filed chromed self-tapping screws (filing to be carried out on opposite sides of the head of the screw so as to produce a cam effect when the screw is turned for adjustment). The screws should be fitted close to the end of the arc of the weights and suitable small holes drilled into the baseplate to allow self-tapping screws to grip. The self-tapper can have the threads cut off to the required length, so as not to protrude through the baseplate, and the threads treated with 'Locktite' or other similar thread lock.

When adjustments are being made to the baseplate, the amount of advance

The baseplate with bobweights and new springs fitted into the distributor body. This picture clearly shows the two different advance springs fitted. At this stage the manual advance/retard mechanism should be set at half distance, to allow for fine-tuning adjustment. It's important that the weights and spring holders are free to move, so all parts should be lightly oiled. When installed, the springs should just be in tension with no slack in at the spring eyes.

can be measured without the springs being fitted. This allows the parts to be moved much more easily.

It's not possible to give the exact spring part numbers that will be required as there are too many variables. However, the standard AC distributor springs are not good enough and allow the weights to advance to their maximum too quickly. At least one much heavier/stronger spring will be required to get the desired results.

It's imperative that, when fitted, the springs are in tension, with absolutely no slack. This is to ensure that the bob weights are kept in the non-advanced position, otherwise the engine will advance very quickly because of the slackness on the advance weights.

To build up a selection of distributor springs a trip to your local breakers' yard will be required. Agree a price for, say, ten distributors before you remove any. Ten different types/ models of distributor will give you a good selection of springs. The normal

price should be around £1 to £2 each.

Spring tension can be adjusted slightly by carefully bending the eyes to give a greater tension.

SOME IMPORTANT POINTS TO REMEMBER

1. The static ignition timing setting should be 10° Before Top Dead Centre (BTDC). There is a mark on the flywheel at 12° Before Top Dead Centre, which is for the valve timing. This mark can be used as a guide when setting the ignition to 10° BTDC. When this is set all the other timing settings at the various revs can then be checked. Small variations in timing can be tolerated at low revs, but should be accurate at higher revs, for example 35° BTDC at 3000rpm is correct.

2. Distributor timing is half the crankshaft timing. Total advance as measured on the distributor (for example 20°) will measure 40° on the crankshaft/flywheel markings. This is because two revolutions of the crankshaft equals one revolution of

the distributor shaft.

3. Different colour timing marks should be painted onto the flywheel so you can distinguish the various changes as the timing advances with increasing engine revs.

4. If the engine advances too quickly shows a reading of 40° when revved to 3000rpm, for example, the distributor bob weight springs are too weak and one should be upgraded.

5. There should be no damage incurred by the engine when carrying out these tests since it's not under load.

VALVES

The original valves are quite satisfactory for a tuned engine and, besides, there isn't enough space to fit larger valve heads. It is possible, though, to fit hardened valve seats and these should be fitted if the opportunity arises so that lead free fuel can be used without the fear of valve seat recession. If replacement or modified valves are used, it's imperative that a check is made that the valve head will pass the top edge of the piston liner. This is particularly important if the compression ratio has been raised.

There is a cutout at the top of the liners to allow the valves to pass, and this should be increased in size to allow for the actual valves being used. A trial run should be carried out, with the valve operation observed from the bottom of the liner, to ensure there is enough clearance. A dummy gasket of the correct thickness should be used when checking these clearances.

If the valves have been ground in

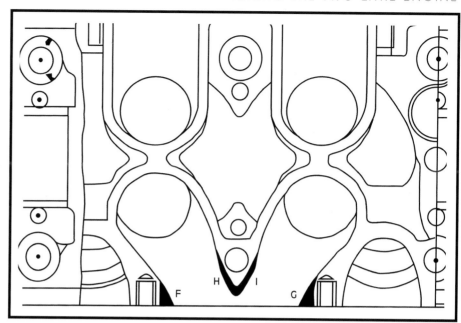

several times, the valve face will tend to sit very deep in the combustion chamber. If this is the case, the edge of the chamber surface, where it meets the valve edge, should be cut down to give as smooth a surface as possible in the combustion chamber.

Drawing A (not to scale). Overhead plan view of the carburettor inlet tracts between manifold and valve head. This drawing shows how much metal can be removed (shaded area). The pointed area at the opening on the inlet should be relieved as shown.

CYLINDER HEAD AND EXHAUST MANIFOLD

Modification of the inlet ports on the AC cylinder head is most important. The original design is quite satisfactory for normal use, of course, but when trying to extract extra power without detriment to reliability the porting becomes very critical.

Producing a good flow for the fuel/air mixture to reach the cylinders is extremely important and there are several specialists who are capable of producing that extra little bit of power from the cylinder head through careful modification.

With regard to the basic AC cylinder head, much can be done to produce a much improved finish to the

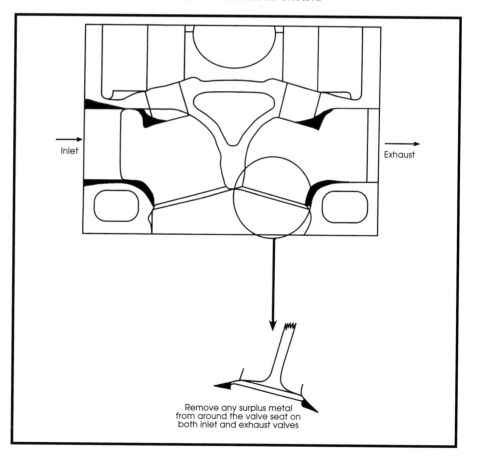

Remove any surplus metal from around the valve seat on both inlet and exhaust valves

Drawing B. This cutaway cross section (viewed from the rear of the engine) shows where and how much metal should be removed from the exhaust & inlet tracts. The dark shaded areas indicate where metal should be removed. The drawing also shows the problem that can occur if the valves have been ground-in several times. A step forms at the edge of the valve opening and this can restrict gas flow. The shaded areas should be removed to ease gasflow.

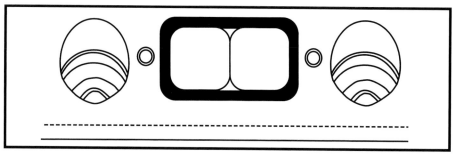

Drawing C (not to scale). This shows a side view of one of the carburettor inlets and the shaded area shows how much metal can be removed from the mouth of the inlet.

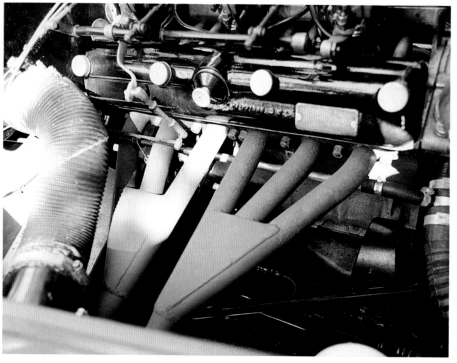

The type of exhaust manifold which is desirable for the AC engine. Two sets of three reducing to one and then both singles joined if convenient.

Remember to cut the carburettor exhaust manifold gaskets to the new enlarged port sizes.

Drawing B shows how the exhaust and inlet tracts in the cylinder head need to be modified. These areas need to be ground as shown to smooth gasflow and provide least resistance. Removing two millimetres from each side at the highest point and smoothing the metal in this area, as per the diagram, will create a much improved gasflow (see also drawing C).

Drawing B also shows where to remove metal from around the valve guide bosses so as to improve gasflow. When all the major metal grinding has taken place within the tracts, all internal surfaces should be finished with fine emery paper to produce a very smooth surface.

Finally, if the inlet and exhaust valves have been ground several times before, there may be a large step built up against the valve edge. This should be ground down and smoothed so as to let the fuel/exhaust gases flow as freely as possible at the opening edges of the valves (see drawing B) but take care not to damage the valve seats.

It's essential to install a six-branch straight pipe exhaust manifold to help the exhaust gases escape quickly, thus improving the combustion process. It is quite satisfactory to have a manifold made where two branches of three lead into two sections and then to one, in a similar fashion to the exhaust manifold on the Bristol 2 litre engines.

VALVE TIMING
The valve timing on the AC engine is

original design.

If you look at Drawing A (not to scale), which is the view from above the cylinder head, you'll see that a large amount of metal can be removed from points F and G where the carburettor manifold joins the cylinder head. It's important that the aluminium carburettor inlet tract is treated in the same way as the cylinder head to create a very smooth passage for the fuel mixture, *e.g.* any shape created by metal removal from the cylinder head

should also be duplicated on the manifold where it joins the cylinder head to maintain a smooth port wall at the joint. It is most important that when removing metal from points H and I, there remains a relatively sharp point in the frontal area. If this area is filed flat, it could cause serious flow deflection. A small amount of metal should be removed from the sides of areas H and I to assist better flow, the drawing highlights where the various stud and casting walls are present.

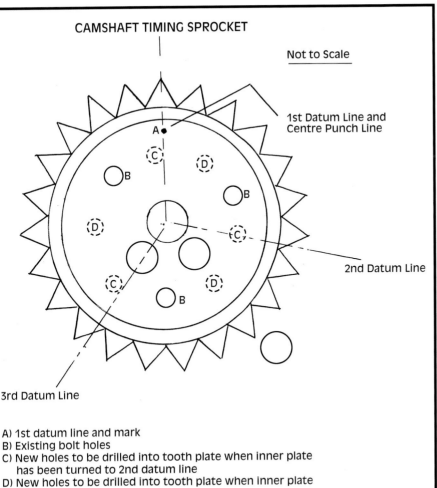

CAMSHAFT TIMING SPROCKET

Not to Scale

1st Datum Line and
Centre Punch Line

2nd Datum Line

3rd Datum Line

A) 1st datum line and mark
B) Existing bolt holes
C) New holes to be drilled into tooth plate when inner plate
   has been turned to 2nd datum line
D) New holes to be drilled into tooth plate when inner plate
   has been turned to 3rd datum line

Once this modification has been carried out, valve timing can be adjusted to within 6° rather than by one tooth which equals 18°. Further minor adjustments can be carried out by adjusting valve clearances to suit the required valve timing.

If, when these adjustments are being made, it's found that number one inlet valve is slow to open when the flywheel is showing the correct 12° marking, a simple adjustment to valve timing can be made by moving the chain on the camshaft sprocket by one tooth. To do this, insert a long thin bar or screwdriver and, by holding the timing chain spring tensioner back, cause the chain to become slack and then make the adjustment. Care should be taken not to let the chain jump a tooth on the crankshaft sprocket when it is slackened. One tooth on the camshaft sprocket equals 18° of crankshaft rotation.

If it's found that adjusting the valve timing by one tooth is too much, the camshaft sprocket can be removed and extra holes drilled in it to facilitate fine timing adjustments. This is carried out by removing the three bolts that hold the two parts of the sprocket together. Note that the sprocket should be marked before disassembly to ensure it can be reassembled in its original state if required. With the bolts removed, the inside section of the sprocket can be rotated one third of a tooth and clamped. New holes should be drilled on the same pitch circle diameter (same distance from the centre of the sprocket) as the existing ones. This should process should be repeated after moving the inside section of the sprocket two thirds of a tooth. Once this modification is complete valve timing can be adjusted by 6° segments, rather than the original 18°.

A very simple method of attaining more power is to set the valve timing

critical for achieving maximum performance and smoothness in the higher rev ranges. There are several ways of adjusting the valve timing, and it's only by experimentation that the maximum performance will be achieved. The standard valve timing for the postwar saloon is that the number one inlet valve should start to open at 12° Before Top Dead Centre (BTDC), with the valve clearances set at 0.020in. As a starting point, slowly turn the engine (with the starting handle, or using a screwdriver on the teeth of the flywheel), in a clockwise direction until the 1/6 timing mark appears on the flywheel. A mark should then be made on the flywheel 1¹/₄in before the 1/6 marking appears. This will give an accurate setting point for

adjusting the valve timing.

One method of setting the valve timing accurately is to adjust number one inlet valve clearance to 0.030in. Turn the engine very slowly as described in the previous paragraph, bringing the new 12° timing mark into view, and insert a 0.010in feeler gauge into the valve clearance gap. When the feeler gauge is nipped and cannot be moved, as the engine is being turned, this signifies that number one inlet valve is just starting to open. Check that the flywheel indicates exactly 12° BTDC. Minor adjustments can be made to the valve clearance to achieve an accurate starting point if the indicator isn't exactly on 12° BTDC. Remember to re-adjust number one valve's clearance back to 0.020in.

accurately to 12° BTDC and then adjust both inlet and exhaust valve clearances to 0.013in. This will allow the engine to breathe a little easier, with just a small loss of low down flexibility.

If the valve clearances are adjusted to 0.013in, it's very important to check that there is enough clearance between the open valve and the cylinder liner and piston crown. If there's any doubt, remove more metal from the liner edge for valve clearance, and cut a small angled groove in the piston crown. This is particularly important with very high compression engines. Do a trial run on the bench, using engineers' putty or Plasticene on the piston crown, to see if the tolerances are acceptable. There's more detail on this testing process in the next section.

CAMSHAFT AND ROCKERS
It is possible to fit a new (high lift) camshaft, but individual requirements would need to be discussed with a camshaft specialist beforehand since the engine should never be revved over 6000rpm.

The standard postwar camshaft had timings of 11-12, 49; 53 and 18°, giving 29° overlap. The last production Two litre engines in the early 1960s had a 54° overlap, and these camshafts timed at 27, 61; 61, 27°. The later camshaft also used a valve clearance setting of .013in (cold). With this later set-up, bhp was definitely increased in the higher rev range, but the engine lost its low down torque and also ran much more roughly.

A very good result will be achieved if a timing of 30, 60; 60, 30° is employed,

giving a duration of 270°. If 0.013in valve clearances are used, valve lift will be increased. It's imperative to check the clearance between the valve and piston crown and this is is best done before the cylinder head is finally tightened down.

The best method of testing is to place engineers' putty or Plasticene 0.040in thick on the surface of number one piston at the points where valve head contact would occur, replace the cylinder head (with an old pre-compressed gasket fitted) and tighten it down. Set the valve timing, rotate the crankshaft a few turns, remove the head and look for any valve head marks on the putty. If the putty has an accurate thickness of 0.040in no marking should occur. To get the putty thickness to 0.040in use a set of feeler gauges and bring together the required amount of gauges to make up 0.040in, place this between two smooth pieces of metal along with the putty and when the pieces of metal are pressed together the putty will have been squeezed to exactly the right size.

If marking is present, the depth should be measured and appropriate grooves cut into the piston surface. A clearance of 0.040in between the piston and valve should always be observed to allow for high revs and clearance adjustments altering valve lift height. If the valve timing of 30, 60; 60, 30 is used, little difference, if any, will be noticed at revs up to 4000rpm. However, over 5000rpm, power gains in the region of 10 per cent can be expected.

The rocker shaft gives good service

and will only need to be replaced if it very worn. The rockers themselves ar rather weak, though, and will break high revs are used. Additiona strengthening metal should be welde to the rockers on the top, bottom an sides where possible, and also onto th ends. Ideally the extra metal should b approximately $^1/_8$in thick. If placed o the top and bottom of the rockers therefore, this will give an overall extr thickness of $^1/_4$in. With thi modification, then, the risk of breakag should be almost eliminated.

The rollers on the ends of th rockers should have no play in then whatsoever, as this will result in furthe stress being put on the ends of th rocker arms, and will make the valv gear noisy. Replacement rollers an pins are readily available.

CARBURETTORS
Most post-war saloons left the factor fitted with three $1^1/_8$in SU carburettors and these give very good and reliabl service. Being such a small carb however, the air flow is rather restricted especially at higher revs. Later AC Ac engines were fitted with three $1^1/_4$in SUs, which improved engine breathing The maximum sized carbs required fo the Two litre AC engine are $1^1/_2$in SUs and these would only be required i revs of over 5500rpm are contemplated

The standard SU needles are DW and the supply of fuel higher in the re range can be improved by the remova of 0.002in from the bottom third o each needle (nearest the point) Thinning the needle here will enrich the mixture higher in the rev range

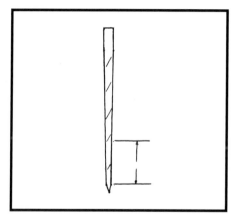

SU DW needle. Remove 0.002in from the area indicated.

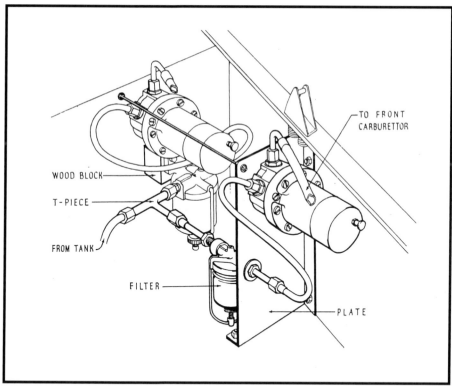

Basic layout showing the plumbing required to install two fuel pumps.

Further gains can be obtained by lengthening the inlet tract, which improves the air wave impulses. The inlet tracts benefit from being lengthened on the engine side of the carb by approximately $2^1/_2$in. Care must be taken that all adjoining surfaces are smooth with no sharp edges. If trumpets are also fitted, this gives a balanced inlet port where the butterfly opening is situated approximately in the middle of the lengthened port.

One thing the AC engine does very easily when modified is to use copious amounts of fuel, especially when using third gear for long periods at high revs. The simple solution is to fit a second fuel pump which feeds to the front carburettor. This will eliminate fuel starvation.

SETTING UP A MODIFIED ENGINE
When the above modifications have been carried out, power output will be greatly improved, and the engine will still give very reliable service.

When all of the modifications have been made to the distributor and the engine, a systematic approach must be taken to setting up and starting the engine so as to allow for final adjustments to the various components that have been changed or modified. All settings should initially be as close to standard as is practical, *e.g.* valve clearances, ignition advance, *etc.*

The first area to concentrate on is the valve timing. Then the carburettors should be tuned to their optimum settings and then concentrate followed by the ignition timing settings. Further small adjustments may be necessary in any or all of these areas to optimise engine performance.

Once the engine has been set up and run until hot, a compression test should be carried out. Even new valves can give trouble and not seat properly giving poor performance, with spitting back and misting fuel vapour showing at the carb inlets. This is best viewed with the filters removed.

A sure sign of incorrect valve timing is the presence of misting fuel vapour at the carb inlets. If this occurs the inlet valves are opening too early and should be adjusted accordingly.

10

DRIVING, MAINTENANCE AND SPARES FOR THE TWO-LITRE

Even today the Two-litre saloon is a practical car to drive in town or on the open road. Performance is adequate and the car will cruise very comfortably at 60-65mph with excellent roadholding. The mechanics and chassis are uncomplicated and home maintenance of the car is within the scope of most enthusiasts. All normal wearing items, such as sparkplugs, points, *etc.*, are readily available, and spares, such as head and engine gaskets, pistons and valves, are all obtainable through the club or from specialists. All engine overhaul work needs to be carried out in a meticulous manner, of course, and any work done to the white metal bearings of the conrods and main bearing caps needs to be carried out to a very high standard if reliability of the engine is to be maintained.

If the engine is in good mechanical condition, it will give many years of good service. In fact, it's the norm for an engine to clock up 75,000 miles before attention is required to the innards.

When testing an engine, it should be run for at least fifteen minutes to warm up. Then listen carefully while revving it to 2000-3000rpm for knocking bearings.

There are a number of main points to look for when purchasing a saloon. The chief concern is rust, of course, especially in the rear sections of the chassis, in the box section next to where the front of the rear springs are attached.

The ash framing of the bodywork was strong but light when these cars were built, but several areas now need to be checked for rot. The screen pillars are a case in point, especially at their bottom edges. If the carpet on the side of the footwell by the door is pulled back, the pillars can be checked by pressing a screwdriver into the timber frame. If soft, it will need to be replaced. With the doors open and the side of the windscreen held firm, there shouldn't be any movement in the scuttle area. If there is, timber replacement work will be needed, which is very time consuming and tricky, requiring removal of the front wings and aluminium bodywork. All the timbers around the rear wheelarches and boot area need to be checked, as does the plywood panelling on the sides of the boot.

A tremendous amount of detailed work has been carried out by an ACOC member, Ian Strange, on the ash framing sections of the body, and very detailed dimensions and drawings are now available. These will be invaluable in restoration if ash framing timbers are missing.

Petrol consumption should be in the region of 22mpg. Maximum speeds through the gears is in the region of: 1st gear – 23mph, 2nd – 45, 3rd – 65, and top 80mph. Quite enough to keep up with today's traffic.

The Moss gearbox is very strong and robust, but good synchromesh was not one of its good points. Going up through the gearbox is normally satisfactory, but changing down at anything more than 20mph in second gear will require double declutching if crunching of the gears is to be avoided.

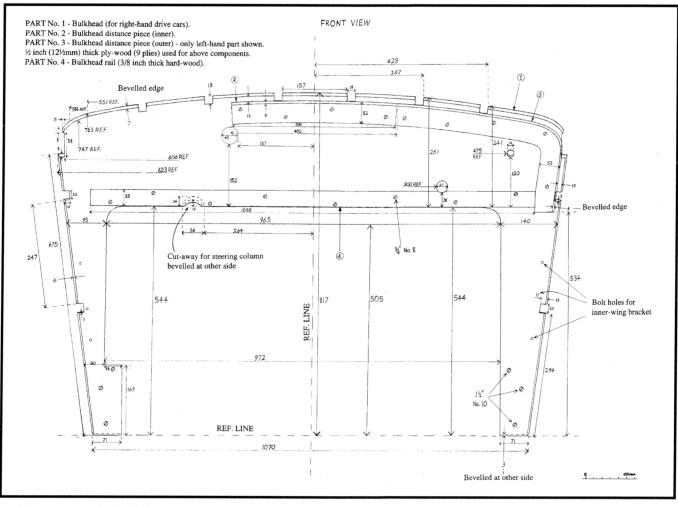

PART No. 1 - Bulkhead (for right-hand drive cars).
PART No. 2 - Bulkhead distance piece (inner).
PART No. 3 - Bulkhead distance piece (outer) - only left-hand part shown.
½ inch (12½mm) thick ply-wood (9 plies) used for above components.
PART No. 4 - Bulkhead rail (3/8 inch thick hard-wood).

The very detailed ash framing drawings which are available from Ian Strange, this one shows the details for the plywood bulkhead.

This all adds to the fun of driving this type of car.

Brakes and all other running gear give very good service, and a well-sorted Two-litre saloon will give years of satisfactory service with normal maintenance.

AC SALOON SPARES CAN BE
OBTAINED FROM SPECIALISTS:
Brian Eacott
12 Lockwood Way
Chessington, KT9 1XX

ACOC Spares Co-ordinator
Clive Bowyer
162 Chesterton Road
Cambridge, CB4 1DA

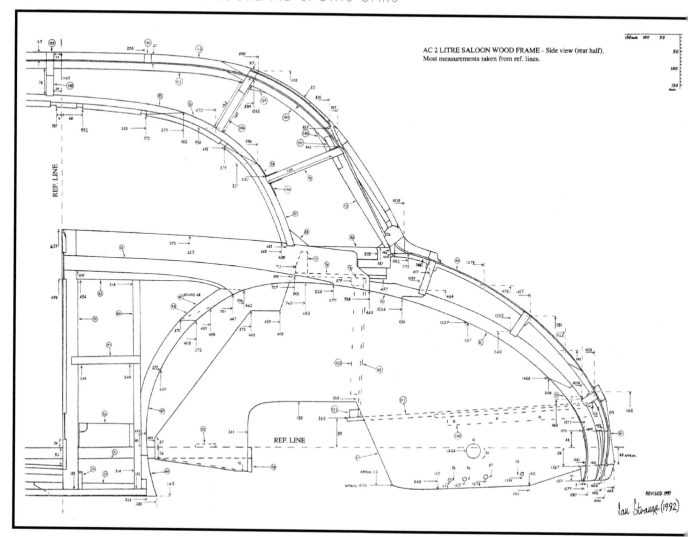

AC 2 LITRE SALOON WOOD FRAME - Side view (rear half).
Most measurements taken from ref. lines.

REVISED 1997

Ian Strange (1992)

Another superbly detailed drawing this time showing a side elevation of the rear of the car.

11

MAIN SPECIFICATION CHANGES TO AC SALOONS

1947
L on the chassis number denotes a final drive unit by the Moss Gear Company.

ELX indicates Export left-hand drive. However, many cars were converted to right-hand drive at the factory.
The rubber surround to the windscreen was changed to a chromed brass frame.

1948
EL 922 ENV back axle introduced alongside the Moss back axle.

L 970 First Drophead Coupé produced.

ELX 1101 16 inch wheels fitted to Drophead.

EL 1127 Buckland introduced.

1949
EL 1149 Two Litre Sports fitted with 7:1 CR pistons.

1949/50
EL 1307 Telescopic shock absorbers replaced lever arm at rear.

1949
EL 1318 Opening rear quarterlight windows fitted.

1950
EL 1403 17 inch wheels replaced by 16 inch wheel rims.
Scuttle air vents fitted

1951
EL 1803 UMB 1802W Metalastic damper fitted to front of crankshaft.

EH 1806 Four-wheel hydraulic brakes fitted.

1952
EH 2020 Four door saloon introduced.

1955
EH 2081 Wire wheels introduced as an option.

EH 2082 CL Ace specification engine replaced UMB.

1958
EH 2095 Last saloon built.

An early specification sheet for the Two-litre.

Chassis and Engine Specifications

CHASSIS FRAME.
Cruciform construction with low centre gravity ensuring amazing road holding ; underslung at rear. Box section for extra rigidity where necessary.

SPRINGS.
Half-elliptic front and rear. Exceptionally resilient, giving exceptional comfort plus wonderful road holding.

SHOCK ABSORBERS.
Front—Woodhead Monroe piston type.
Rear—Girling hydraulic with pressure recuperation.

CHASSIS LUBRICATION.
Grease nipples.

ENGINE.
16/74 H.P. has been produced after years of experiment and proved dependability, and is fitted to all models. It is a six-cylinder monobloc water-cooled with detachable head. Bore and stroke 65 by 100 mm., cubic capacity 1,991 c.c. Crankshaft carried on five bearings, overhead valves, pressure lubrication through adequate filters from gear pump submerged in sump ; capacity of sump 1¾ gallons. Camshaft chain kept taut by patent spring tensioner. Cast cylinder liners, cooling water completely surrounds liners over entire working surface. Vibration damper and special rubber mounting giving freedom from vibration and maximum silence. Engine compression ratio—6½ : 1. Develops 74 b.h.p. at 4,500 r.p.m.

CARBURETTERS.
Three S.U. carburetters with special S.U. automatic easy starting device.

CAMSHAFT.
Overhead, driven by Duplex roller chain. Eccentric base cams give definitely quiet tappets.

CRANKSHAFT.
Statically and dynamically balanced. Five bearings. Damping device fitted.

CLUTCH.
Borg and Beck single dry-plate, totally enclosed in flywheel, having exceptionally smooth action combined with positive drive under full load. The type of clutch used needs no attention whatever.

COOLING.
Pump and fan with thermostat control. New design of radiator gives exceptional driving visibility.

GEARBOX.
4-speed central lever. Synchromesh on second, third and top gears.

	Top.	3rd.	2nd.	1st.	Reverse.
Ratios :—	4.625 : 1	6.32 : 1	9.16 : 1	15.6 : 1	15.6 : 1

PROPELLOR SHAFT.
Hardy Spicer needle type. Balanced to ensure smooth running.

REAR AXLE.
Hypoid spiral bevel gears give a permanently silent drive and obviates high propellor shaft tunnel. Semi-floating. Tapered roller-bearings throughout.

FRONT AXLE.
H-section ; steel forging with rounded ends to withstand severe braking.

BRAKES.
Girling 12″ hydra-mechanical, giving very powerful progressive braking with light pedal pressure.

STEERING GEAR.
Self-centering, light and positive in action ; simple method of adjustment to take up play in cam worm. 40 ft. turning circle. Bluemels spring spoke wheel with adjustable steering column.

ELECTRICAL SYSTEM.
Lucas 12-volt light and starting system, automatic voltage control ; double arm windscreen wiper ; headlamps, operated by foot dipper switch ; two "Stop" lights operated by brake pedal ; self-cancelling direction indicators ; dual wind-tone horns ; 12-volt battery capacity 60 amp./10 hrs., 69 amp./20 hrs. Illuminated instrument board.

INSTRUMENTS.
5″ speedometer incorporating electric clock ; 5″ panel combining the following instruments : Oil gauge, thermometer, petrol gauge and ammeter.

PETROL SYSTEM.
Petrol supply by S.U. pump from rear-mounted 11½ gallon petrol tank. Special filter in main feed line. Gauge on dash.

TYRES.
17 x 5.50.

WHEELS.
Dunlop steel disc with chromium cap.

WHEEL TRACK.
55″.

WHEEL BASE.
117″.

ROAD CLEARANCE.
7″.

JACKS.
Smith's "Bevelift" type.

BODY.
Built complete at our Works. Finest seasoned wood framing—panelled in 18 gauge aluminium. Mudguards 16 gauge aluminium.

SAFETY GLASS.
All round.

BODY INTERIOR DIMENSIONS.

Seat to roof	F.	36″
	R.	35″
Width over seat at elbow	F.	52½″
	R.	53″
Width between armrests		44″
Height of seat from floor	F.	12″
	R.	14″
Leg room, max.	F.	38½″ Back of squab to pedals.
	R.	36½″ Back of rear squab to front seat.
Door width at waistline	F.	41″
Luggage container	H.	18½″
	W.	44″
	D.	26½″

OVERALL LENGTH OF CAR.
184″.

OVERALL WIDTH OF CAR.
67″.

WEIGHT OF COMPLETE CAR.
25 cwt. approximately.

In view of the present difficulties regarding supplies of materials, we reserve the right to alter the foregoing specification.

A.C. CARS LTD., THAMES DITTON, SURREY

12

TOOL KIT SPECIFICATION

Spanners (Carrington Merlin)
all Whitworth -
$^1/_2$in & $^7/_{16}$in
$^7/_{16}$in & $^3/_8$in
$^5/_{16}$in & $^1/_4$in
$^3/_{16}$in & $^1/_8$in
Sparkplug spanner

Spark plug T-bar (centre punch)
Box spanner $^3/_{16}$in Whitworth
Screwdriver 8in
Hub cap remover
Bonnet lock key
Pliers
Wheelbrace

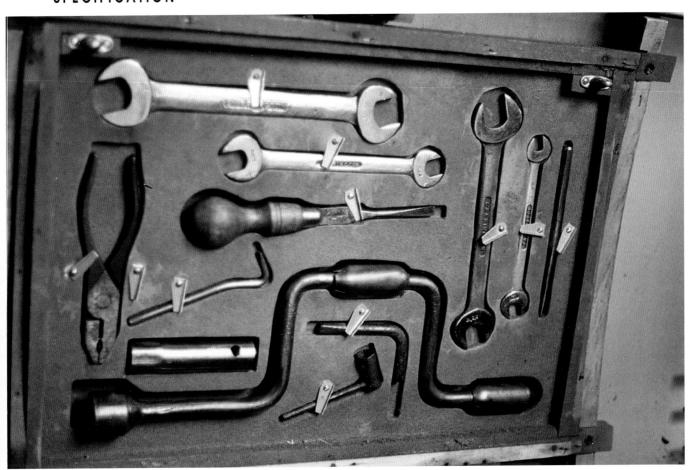

On the saloon the complete tool kit is kept behind a hinged door in the boot lid.

The jack and starting handle are held by clips in the boot and the grease gun is clipped to the inside wing panel on the carburettor side of the engine.

APPENDIX:
CHASSIS RECORDS

2 Dr	two-door
Protp	Prototype
SP S C	Special short chassis
4 Dr	4 door
LX	Export model
2L SP T	2 litre sports tourer
DHC	Drophead coupe
N/A	Information not available
UNP	Unpainted
Exprtl	Experimental
Buckl	Buckland
RHD	Right hand drive
LHD	Left hand drive

All cars are two-door unless otherwise stated
All car engine numbers start with UMB unless otherwise stated.

The following information is given to help identify each car. However, the factory records are not very clear. Some chassis are stated to have been sent to coachbuilders with wings only. It would be expected that different body styles and finishes would be present in surviving cars, but on close inspection some cars sent as chassis and wings only appear to be exactly as the factory finished cars, including the leather interior. Whether some of these chassis were returned to the factory is not clear as no mention of this is recorded in the factory records.

First reg	Body type	Body colour	Interior colour	Chassis no.	Engine no.	Comments
1946	Exprtl DHC	Black	Beige	L800	800	1939 body fitted to 2 litre chassis
1947	Protp	Grey	Beige	L801	801	
1947		Grey	Beige	L802	803	
1947		Grey	Beige	LX803	802	RHD (Switzerland)
1947		Grey	Beige	LX804	806	RHD (Belgium)
1948		Grey	Blue	L805	823	Australia

First reg	Body type	Body colour	Interior colour	Chassis no.	Engine no.	Comments
1947		Grey	Beige	LX806	804	RHD (Switzerland)
1947		Grey	Beige	L807	807	Uruguay
1947		Grey	Beige	LX808	808	RHD (Norway)
1947		Grey	Beige	LX809	809	LHD (Switzerland)
1947		Black	Red	L810	810	
1947		Grey	Beige	LX811	811	RHD (Madeira)
1947		Grey	Blue	L812	805	Australia
1947		Black	Red	L813	812	RHD (Singapore)
1947		Grey	Beige	L814	813	RHD (Sweden)
1947		Grey	Beige	L815	814	RHD (Sweden)
1948		Black	Beige	L816	815	
1948		Grey	Blue	L817	816	
1948		Grey	Beige	L818	818	
1948		Grey	Beige	L819	817	
1948		Black	Red	LX820	819	LHD (Brazil)
1948		Grey	Blue	L821	821	
1948		Grey	Red	LX822	824	LHD (Uruguay)
1948		Grey	Red	LX823	820	LHD (Switzerland)
1948		Black	Red	LX824	827	LHD
1948		Grey	Beige	LX825	828	LHD (Brazil)
1948		Grey	Beige	LX826	825	LHD (Switzerland)
1948		Grey	Beige	LX827	826	
1948		Grey	Blue	LX828	829	LHD (Brazil)
1948		Grey	Beige	L829	833	
1948		Grey	Beige	LX830	831	LHD
1948		Grey	Blue	L831	832	
1948		Grey	Blue	L832	834	
1948		Grey	Beige	LX833	835	RHD
1948		Black	Red	LX834	830	LHD
1948		Black	Beige	LX835	836	LHD
1948		Grey	Red	LX836	837	LHD (Switzerland)

First reg	Body type	Body colour	Interior colour	Chassis no.	Engine no.	Comments
N/A	N/A	N/A	N/A	L837X	N/A	Yorkshire
1948		Grey	Blue	LX838	839	LHD
1948		Grey	Beige	L839	840	
1948		Grey	Beige	L840	841	
1948		Grey	Blue	LX841	842	LHD
1949		Black	Red	L842X	843	LHD
1948		Grey	Beige	L843	844	
1948		UNP	Red	LX844	845	LHD
1948		Grey	Red	LX845	846	LHD
1948		Grey	Red	L846	847	
1948		Grey	Beige	L847	848	EIRE
1948		Grey	Red	EL848	849	
1948		Grey	Blue	L849	850	RHD (Malta)
1948		Grey	Blue	L850	851	
1949		Grey	Beige	LX851	852	
1948	DHC	Grey	Beige	L852	876	First exprtl
1949		Black	Red	L853X	N/A	
1949		N/A	N/A	EL854X	N/A	
1949	DHC	Grey	Beige	ELX855	885	LHD (Geneva)
1948		Grey	Red	L856	853	
1948		Black	Red	L857	854	
1948		UNP	Beige	L858	855	
1948		UNP	Beige	L859	856	
1948		UNP	Red	L860	857	
1948		Grey	Beige	L861	858	
1948		Grey	Beige	L862	859	
1948		Grey	Blue	L863	860	
1948		Grey	Beige	L864	861	
1948		Grey	Red	L865	862	
1948		Blue	Blue	LX866	897	LHD
1949		Grey	Beige	LX867	898	LHD
1948		Grey	Blue	L868	971	
1948		UNP	Grey	L869	974	
1948		Black	Beige	L870	975	
1948		Bronze	Brown	L871	863	Cloth upholstery
1948		Black	Beige	L872	864	
1948		Black	Beige	L873	865	
1948		Black	Red	L874	866	
1948		Grey	Blue	L875	867	

First reg	Body type	Body colour	Interior colour	Chassis no.	Engine no.	Comments
948		UNP	Beige	L876	868	
948		Grey	Beige	L877	869	
948		UNP	Beige	L878	870	
948		Black	Beige	L879	871	
948		Grey	Beige	L880	872	
948		Grey	Red	L881	874	
948		Grey	Beige	L882	875	
948		Grey	Red	L883	873	
948		UNP	Red	L884	877	
948		UNP	Beige	L885	878	
948		Grey	Red	L886	879	
948		Black	Red	L887	880	
948		UNP	Grey	L888	881	
948		UNP	Beige	L889	882	
948		Grey	Red	L890	886	
948		Grey	Red	L891	887	
948		Grey	Grey	L892	888	
948		Grey	Beige	L893	889	
948		Black	Red	L894	890	
948		Grey	Beige	L895	891	
948		Grey	Red	L896	892	
948		Black	Red	L897	893	
948		Grey	Beige	L898	894	
948		Grey	Blue	L899	895	
948		Grey	Red	L900	896	
948		Grey	Beige	L901	899	
948		Grey	Red	L902	900	
1948		Beige	Red	L903	901	Jersey
1948		Grey	Red	L904	902	
1948		Black	Red	L905	903	
1948		Grey	Beige	L906	904	
1948		Grey	Grey	L907	905	
1948		Grey	Beige	L908	906	
1948		Grey	Grey	L909	907	
1948		Grey	Grey	L910	908	
1948		Grey	Beige	L911	909	
1948		Black	Beige	L912	910	
1948				L913	911	Chassis only
1948				L914	912	Chassis only
1948				L915	913	Chassis only
1948		Black	Red	L916	915	
1948				L917	914	Chassis only

First reg	Body type	Body colour	Interior colour	Chassis no.	Engine no.	Comments
						W wings
1948				L918	917	Chassis only W wings
1948		Grey	Beige	L919	916	
1948		Grey	Beige	L920	918	
1948		N/A	N/A	L921	920	AC demo car
1948				L922	919	AC demo car env rear axle fitted – now EL922
1949				L923	921	Chassis only W wings
1948				L924	922	Chassis only W wings
1948		Black	Beige	L925	923	
1948		Grey	Red	L926	924	
1948		Black	Red	L927	925	
1948		Grey	Grey	L928	926	
1948		Grey	Beige	L929	927	
1948				L930	928	Chassis only W wings
1948		Grey	Red	L931	929	
1948		Grey	Red	L932	930	
1948		Black	Beige	L933	931	Belfast
1948				L934	932	Chassis only W wings
1948		Black	Beige	L935	933	
1948		Black	Beige	L936	934	
1948		Grey	Red	L937	935	
1948		Grey	Blue	L938	936	
1948				L939	937	Chassis only
1948		Grey	Beige	L940	938	
1948		Grey	Grey	L941	939	
1948		Grey	Grey	L942	941	
1948		Grey	Beige	L943	942	
1948		Black	Beige	L944	944	
1948		UNP	Beige	L945	945	
1948		Grey	Blue	L946	946	
1948		Grey	Beige	L947	947	
1948		Grey	Grey	L948	948	
1948		Grey	Beige	L949	949	
1948		UNP	Grey	L950	951	

First reg	Body type	Body colour	Interior colour	Chassis no.	Engine no.	Comments
1948		Black	Beige	L951	952	
1948		Grey	Beige	L952	954	
1948		Black	Beige	L953	953	
1948		Black	Beige	L954	954	
1948		Grey	Grey	L955	955	
1948				L956	956	Chassis only W wings
1948				L957	957	Chassis only W wings
1948		Black	Beige	L958	958	
1948		UNP	Grey	L959	960	
1948		UNP	Beige	L960	961	
1948		Grey	Beige	L961	N/A	Isle of Man
1948		Black	Beige	L962	N/A	
1948		Grey	Blue	L963	964	
1948		UNP	Grey	L964	N/A	
1948		Beige	Red	L965	966	
1948		Blue	Blue	L966	943	
1948		Grey	Beige	L967	967	
1948		Grey	Blue	L968	968	
1949	DHC	Grey	Beige	L969	969	
1949	DHC	Grey	Beige	L970	970	Beige hood
1948		Grey	Beige	EL971	973	
1948		Grey	Beige	L972	972	
1948		Grey	Blue	L973	976	
1948		Grey	Beige	EL974	977	
1948		Grey	Blue	EL975	978	
1948		Grey	Red	EL976	940	
1948		Black	Beige	EL977	979	
1948		Grey	Beige	EL978	980	
1948				L979	981	Chassis only W wings
1948		Grey	Red	L980	959	
1948		UNP	Blue	L981	982	
1948		Grey	Blue	L982	983	
1948		Grey	Red	L983	984	
1948		Grey	Grey	L984	986	
1948				L985	988	Chassis only W wings
1948		Grey	Beige	L986	987	
1948		Grey	Beige	L987	989	
1948		Grey	Grey	L988	990	

First reg	Body type	Body colour	Interior colour	Chassis no.	Engine no.	Comments
1948		Grey	Grey	L989	991	
1948				L990	992	Chassis only
1948		Grey	Grey	L991	993	
1948		Grey	Grey	L992	994	
1948		Grey	Grey	L993	995	
1948		Grey	Grey	L994	996	
1948		Grey	Grey	L995	997	
1948		Grey	Beige	L996	998	
1948		Grey	Beige	L997	999	
1948		Grey	Grey	L998	1000	
1948		Grey	Grey	L999	1001	
1948		Blue	Blue	EL1000	1003	
1948		Black	Red	EL1001	1004	
1948		Grey	Beige	EL1002	1005	
1948		Grey	Beige	EL1003	1006	
1948		Grey	Grey	EL1004	1007	
1948		Grey	Grey	EL1005	1008	
1948		Grey	Beige	EL1006	1010	
1948		Grey	Red	EL1007	1011	
1948		Grey	Red	EL1008	1012	
1948		Black	Beige	EL1009	1013	
1948		Grey	Red	EL1010	1014	
1949		Black	Beige	EL1011	1035	
1948		Grey	Red	EL1012	1015	
1948		Blue	Blue	EL1013	1016	
1948		Grey	Red	EL1014	1017	
1949		Grey	Red	EL1015	1020	
1948		Grey	Red	EL1016	1018	
1948		Grey	Beige	EL1017	1041	demo car
1949		Grey	Red	L1018	985	
1949		Grey	Red	L1019	1021	
1949				L1020	N/A	Chassis only
1949		Grey	Red	L1021	1023	
1949		Grey	Red	L1022	1019	
1949				L1023	1024	Chassis only
1949		Grey	Red	L1024	1025	
1949		Grey	Beige	L1025	1026	
1949		Black	Red	L1026	1027	
1949		Grey	Beige	EL1027	1028	
1948				EL1028	1029	Chassis only
1949		Grey	Red	EL1029	1030	
1949		Black	Beige	EL1030	1031	

First reg	Body type	Body colour	Interior colour	Chassis no.	Engine no.	Comments
1949		Grey	Red	EL1031	1032	
1949		Grey	Red	EL1032	1033	
1949		Grey	Beige	EL1033	1034	
1949		Black	Beige	EL1034	1036	
1949		Grey	Beige	EL1035	1037	
1948				EL1036	1038	Chassis only Front wings First Buckland
1949		Grey	Red	EL1037	1039	
1949		Grey	Beige	EL1038	1040	
1949		Grey	Beige	EL1039	1042	
1948				EL1040	1043	Chassis only
1949		Black	Beige	EL1041	1044	
1949		Grey	Beige	EL1042	1045	
1949		Black	Beige	EL1043	1046	
1949		Black/ Green?	Beige	EL1044	1100	
1949		Grey	Beige	EL1045	1048	
1949		Grey	Beige	EL1046	1049	
1949		Grey	Blue	EL1047	1050	
1949		Grey	Red	EL1048	N/A	
1949		Beige	Red	EL1049	1052	
1949		Grey	Grey	EL1050	1053	
1949		Grey	Grey	EL1051	1054	
1949		Grey	Blue	EL1052	1055	
1949		Grey	Red	EL1053	1056	
1949		Grey	Red	EL1054	1057	
1949		Grey	Blue	EL1055	1058	
1949		Grey	Blue	EL1056	1059	
1949		Grey	Blue	EL1057	1060	
1949		Grey	Beige	EL1058	1061	
1949		Grey	Beige	EL1059	1062	
1949		Grey	Beige	EL1060	1063	
1949		Grey	Grey	EL1061	1064	
1949		Grey	Grey	EL1062	1065	
1949		Grey	Grey	EL1063	1066	
1949		Grey	Beige	EL1064	1067	
1949		Black	Beige	EL1065	1068	
1949		Black	Beige	EL1066	1101	
1949		Grey	Beige	EL1067	1069	
1949		Black	Beige	EL1068	1071	Belfast
1949		Grey	Beige	EL1069	1070	RHD (Switzerland)
1949		Grey	Grey	EL1070	1072	
1949		Grey	Grey	EL1071	1073	
1949		Grey	Grey	EL1072	1074	
1949		Grey	Grey	EL1073	1075	
1949		Grey	Grey	EL1074	1076	
1949		Grey	Grey	EL1075	1095	
1949				EL1076	1078	Chassis only
1949				L1077	1079	Chassis only
1949		Beige	Red	L1078	1080	
1949		Grey	Grey	L1079	1081	
1949		Beige	Red	L1080	1111	
1949		Black	Red	L1081	1109	
1949		Black	Red	L1082	N/A	
1949		Grey	Blue	L1083	1083	
1949		Grey	Grey	L1084	1084	
1949		Grey	Blue	L1085	1085	
1949		Grey	Blue	L1086	1086	
1949		Grey	Blue	L1087	1087	
1949		Grey	Beige	L1088	1088	
1949		Grey	Beige	EL1089	1089	
1949		Black	Beige	EL1090	1090	
1949		Grey	Beige	EL1091	1091	
1949		Black	Beige	EL1092	1077	Isle of Man
1949		Black	Red	L1093	1092	
1949		Black	Red	EL1094	1093	
1949		Grey	Red	EL1095	822	
1949		Grey	Red	EL1096	1094	AC demo car
1949		Black	Red	EL1097	1096	
1949		Grey	Beige	EL1098	1097	
1949		Grey	Beige	EL1099	1098	
1949		Grey	Beige	EL1100	1099	
1949		Blue	Blue	ELX1101	1102	LDH (Uruguay?)
1950	DHC	N/A	N/A	ELX1102	1103	LHD (Holland)
1949	UNP	Beige		EL1103	1104	
1949		Grey	Grey	EL1104	1105	
1949		Grey	Grey	EL1105	1107	
1949		Grey	Grey	EL1106	1108?	
1949		Grey	Grey	EL1107	1047	

First reg	Body type	Body colour	Interior colour	Chassis no.	Engine no.	Comments
1949		Grey	Grey	EL1108	1108?	
1949		Blue	Blue	EL1109	1110	
1949		Grey	Blue	EL1110	1113	
1949		Grey	Blue	EL1111	1112	
1949		Grey	Blue	EL1112	1114	
1949		Grey	Blue	L1113	1115	
1949		Black	Beige	EL1114	1116	
1949		Grey	Beige	EL1115	1117	
1949		Black	Beige	EL1116	1118	
1949		Black	Beige	EL1117	1119	
1949		Grey	Beige	L1118	1120	
1949		Grey	Grey	L1119	1121	
1949		Grey	Grey	L1120	1123	
1949		Grey	Grey	L1121	1122	
1949		Grey	Grey	L1122	1125	
1949		Grey	Grey	L1123	1126	
1949		Black	Red	L1124	1132	
1949		Black	Red	L1125	1127	
1949		Grey	Red	EL1126	1128	
1949	Buckl	N/A	N/A	EL1127	1124	Chassis only
1949		Beige	Red	EL1128	1131	
1949		Grey	Beige	EL1129	1129	
1949		Black	Beige	EL1130	1133	
1949		Black	Red	EL1131	1134	
1949		Black	Beige	EL1132	1130	Belfast
1949		Black	Beige	EL1133	1135	
1949		Grey	Beige	EL1134	1136	
1949		Grey	Grey	EL1135	1137	
1949		Grey	Grey	EL1136	1138	
1949		Grey	Grey	EL1137	1141	
1949		Grey	Grey	EL1138	1142	
1949		Grey	Grey	EL1139	1145	
1949		Blue	Blue	EL1140	1144	
N/A	Buckl	Cream	Red	ELX1141	1289	USA
1950		N/A	N/A	ELX1142	1312	LHD (Montevideo)
1950	Buckl	N/A	N/A	ELX1143	1153	LHD
1949		Blue	Blue	ELX1144	1145	LHD
1950	DHC	Grey	Beige	ELX1145	1355	Uruguay
1949		Grey	Grey	EL1146	1147	
1949		Grey	Blue	EL1147	1151	
1949		Grey	Beige	EL1148	1152	

First reg	Body type	Body colour	Interior colour	Chassis no.	Engine no.	Comments
1949	Buckl	N/A	N/A	EL1149	1149	
1949		Grey	Blue	EL1150	1153	
1949		Blue	Blue	EL1151	1154	
1949		Blue	Blue	EL1152	1155	
1949		Grey	Red	EL1153	1156	
1949		Beige	Red	EL1154	1157	
1949		Black	Red	EL1155	1158	
1950	Exprtl	Grey	Red	EL1156	1319	Upswept chassis
1949		Black	Red	EL1157	1159	
1949		Black	Beige	EL1158	1161	
1949		Beige	Red	EL1159	1162	
1949		Black	Beige	EL1160	1163	
1949		Black	Beige	EL1161	1164	
1949		Black	Beige	EL1162	1165	
1949		Black	Beige	EL1163	1165	
1949		Grey	Grey	EL1164	1167	
1949		Grey	Grey	EL1165	1168	
1949		Grey	Grey	EL1166	1169	
1949		Grey	Blue	EL1167	1170	
1949		Grey	Grey	EL1168	1172	
1949		Grey	Blue	EL1169	1174	
1949		Grey	Blue	EL1170	1171	
1949		Grey	Blue	EL1171	1175	
1949		Blue	Blue	EL1172	1176	
1949		Grey	Beige	EL1173	1177	
1949		Grey	Beige	EL1174	1179	
1949		Grey	Beige	L1175	1178	
1949		Grey	Beige	L1176	1180	
1949		Black	Beige	L1177	1181	
1949		Black	Red	L1178	1182	
1949		Grey	Red	L1179	1183	
1949		Grey	Red	L1180	1186	
1949	Buckl	Blue	Cream	EL1181	1150	
1949		Grey	Red	EL1182	1184	
1949		Grey	Blue	EL1183	1185	
1949		Black	Red	EL1184	1187	
1949		Grey	Blue	EL1185	1188	
1949		Grey	Blue	EL1186	1189	
1949		Grey	Blue	EL1187	1160	
1949		Grey	Blue	EL1188	1190	
1949		Grey	Beige	L1189	1191	

First reg	Body type	Body colour	Interior colour	Chassis no.	Engine no.	Comments
949		Black	Beige	EL1190	1192	
949		Grey	Beige	EL1191	1193	
949		Grey	Beige	EL1192	1194	
949		Grey	Beige	EL1193	1139	
949		Beige	Red	EL1194	1195	
949		Grey	Red	L1195	1196	
949		Grey	Red	EL1196	1197	Isle of Man
949		Grey	Red	EL1197	1198	
949		Grey	Beige	EL1198	1173	
949		Grey	Red	EL1199	1199	
949		Black	Beige	EL1200	1200	
949		Black	Beige	EL1201	1201	
949		Black	Beige	L1202	1203	
949		Grey	Red	EL1203	1204	
949		Grey	Beige	EL1204	1202	Belfast
949	Buckl			EL1205	1148/7	
949		Grey	Red	EL1206	1206	
949		Grey	Red	EL1207	1205	
949		Grey	Red	EL1208	1208	
949		Grey	Beige	L1209	1210	
949		Black	Red	EL1210	1207	Isle of Man
949		Grey	Beige	EL1211	1209	
949		Grey	Beige	EL1212	1212	
949		Black	Beige	EL1213	1211	
949		Grey	Beige	EL1214	1214	
949		Grey	Red	EL1215	1213	
949		Grey	Red	EL1216	1216	
949		Grey	Red	EL1217	1215	
949		Grey	Red	1218	1218	
949		Grey	Red	EL1219	1217	
949		Black	Beige	L1220	1220	
949		Grey	Beige	L1221	1219	
949		Grey	Beige	EL1222	1222	
949		Grey	Beige	EL1223	1224	
949		Black	Beige	EL1224	1221	
949		Grey	Red	EL1225	1223	
949		Black	Red	EL1226	1225	
949		Grey	Red	EL1227	1227	
		N/A	N/A	N/A	1228	N/A
949		Grey	Red	EL1229	1228	
949		Blue	Blue	EL1230	1229	
949		Blue	Blue	EL1231	1231	

First reg	Body type	Body colour	Interior colour	Chassis no.	Engine no.	Comments
1949		Grey	Beige	EL1232	1230	
1949		Grey	Beige	EL1233	1232	
1949		Black	Beige	EL1234	1233	
1949		Grey	Red	EL1235	1235	
1949		Grey	Red	EL1236	1236	
1949	Buckl	Cream	Red	EL1237	1146	
1949		Black	Red	EL1238	1242	
1949		Grey	Red	EL1239	1238	
1949		Grey	Red	EL1240	1239	
1949		Blue	Blue	EL1241	1241	
1949		Grey	Beige	EL1242	1240	
1949		Black	Beige	EL1243	1246	
1950	DHC	Grey	Beige	EL1244	1244	
1949		Grey	Beige	EL1245	1244	
1949		Grey	Red	EL1246	1245	
1950		DHC	Grey	Red	EL1247 1248	
1949	Buckl	EL1248			1247	
1949		N/A	N/A	EL1249	1249	
1950	DHC	Grey	Red	EL1250	1250	
1949		Grey	Red	EL1251	1251	
1950	DHC	Grey	Beige	EL1252	N/A	
1949		UNP	Red	EL1253	1253	
1949	DHC?	Grey	Red	EL1254	1254	
1949		Grey	Beige	EL1255	1255	
1949		Grey	Beige	EL1256	1256	
1949		Grey	Red	EL1257	1257	
1949		Grey	Beige	L1258	1140	
1949		Grey	Beige	L1259	1260	
1949		Grey	Red	EL1260	1258	
1949	Buckl	N/A	N/A	EL1261	1261	
1949		Grey	Red	EL1262	1263	
1949		Grey	Red	EL1263	1268?	
1949		Black	Beige	EL1264	1262	Belfast
1949		Grey	Red	EL1265	1264	
1949		Grey	Beige	EL1266	1266	
1949		Grey	Red	EL1267	1267	
1949		Grey	Beige	EL1268	1268?	Belfast
1949		Grey	Beige	1269	1269	
1949		Black	Beige	EL1270	1270	
1949		N/A	N/A	EL1271	N/A	
1949		Grey	Red	EL1272	1259	
1949	Buckl	N/A	N/A	EL1273	1275	

First reg	Body type	Body colour	Interior colour	Chassis no.	Engine no.	Comments
N/A	Saloon	N/A	N/A	EL1274	N/A	
1949		Grey	Red	EL1275	N/A	
1949	Saloon?	Black	Red	EL1276	1274	
1949		Cream	Red	EL1277	1276	
1949		Black	Beige	EL1278	1278	
1949		Grey	Beige	EL1279	1277	
1949		Grey	Beige	EL1280	1279	
1949		Grey	Beige	EL1281	1280	
1949		Grey	Beige	EL1282	1283	
1949	Buckl			EL1283	1281	
1950		Grey	Red	EL1284	1282	
1949		Black	Red	L1285	1237	
1949		Black	Red	EL1286	1284	
1949		Grey	Red	EL1287	1285	
1949		Grey	Red	EL1288	1291	
1949		Grey	Red	EL1289	1288	
1949		Grey	Red	EL1290	1287	
1949		Grey	Red	EL1291	1292	
1950		Black	Red	EL1292	1293	
1950		Grey	Blue	L1293	1294	
1950		Grey	Blue	L1294	1295	
1949		Grey	Red	L1295	1296	
1950		Grey	Blue	L1296	1297	
1950		Grey	Blue	L1297	1298	
1950		Grey	Blue	L1298	1288	
1950		Black	Beige	EL1299	1300A	
1950		Black	Beige	L1300	1299	
1950		Black	Beige	L1301	1300	
1950		Grey	Blue	L1302	1300B	
1949	?			EL1303	1290	Chassis only
1950		Grey	Beige	EL1304	1301	
1950		UNP	Beige	EL1305	1302	
1950		Grey	Blue	EL1306	1303	
1950		Grey	Blue	EL1307	1304	
1950		Grey	Blue	EL1308	1305	
1950		Grey	Red	EL1309	1306	
1950		Black	Beige	EL1310	1307	Belfast
1950		Black	Red	EL1311	1308	
1950		Black	Red	EL1312	1309	
1950		Grey	Red	EL1313	1310	
1950		Black	Beige	EL1314	1311	
1950		Grey	Beige	EL1315	1313	
1950		Black	Beige	EL1316	1314	
1950		N/A	N/A	EL1317	1315	Owned by George Formby
1950		Blue	Blue	EL1318	1316	
1950		Grey	Blue	EL1319	1317	
1950		Grey	Blue	EL1320	1318	
1950		Grey	Blue	EL1321	1320	
1950		Grey	Blue	EL1322	1321	
1950		Black	Red	EL1323	1322	
1950		Grey	Red	EL1324	1323	
1950		Grey	Red	EL1325	1324	
1950		Black	Red	EL1326	1325	
1949	Buckl			EL1327	1329	
1950	Buckl			EL1328	1330	
1950		Black	Beige	EL1329	1326	
1950		Grey	Beige	EL1330	1327	
1950		UNP	Beige	EL1331	1328	
1950		Grey	Beige	EL1332	1331	
1950		Black	Beige	EL1333	1332	
1950		Grey	Red	EL1334	1333	
1950		Grey	Beige	EL1335	1334	
1950		Black	Red	EL1336	1335	Isle of Man
1950		Grey	Red	EL1337	1336	
1950	Buckl			EL1338	1338	
1950		Black	Red	EL1339	1339	
1950		Grey	Red	EL1340	1340	
1950	SP S C			EL1341	1337	Buckland Bodyworks
1950		Grey	Red	EL1342	1347	
1950		Grey	Red	ELX1343	1342	
1950		Grey	Red	EL1344	1346	
1950		Grey	Red	EL1345	1345	
1950		Grey	Blue	EL1346	1344	
1950		Blue	Blue	EL1347	1343	
1950		Blue	Blue	EL1348	1348	
1950		Grey	Blue	EL1349	1349	
1950	Buckland	N/A	N/A	EL1350	1352	
1950		Grey	Blue	EL1351	1350	
1950		Black	Beige	EL1352	1351	
1950		Grey	Beige	EL1353	1341	
1950		Black	Beige	EL1354	1354	

First reg	Body type	Body colour	Interior colour	Chassis no.	Engine no.	Comments
1950		Black	Beige	EL1355	1356	
1950		Black	Beige	EL1356	1358	
1950		Grey	Red	EL1357	1357	
1950		Black	Red	EL1358	1360	
1950		Grey	Red	EL1359	1363	
1950		Grey	Red	ELX1360	N/A	Uruguay
1950		Black	Red	EL1361	1364	Belfast
1950		Grey	Blue	EL1362	1365	
1950		Blue	Blue	EL1363	1366	
1950		Grey	Blue	EL1364	1368	Isle of Man
1950		Grey	Blue	EL1365	1367	
1950		Grey	Blue	EL1366	1370	
1950	Buckl			EL1367	1361	
1950		Grey	Beige	EL1368	1369	
1950		Grey	Beige	EL1369	1373	
1950		Grey	Beige	EL1370	1439	
1950		Black	Beige	EL1371	1376	
1950		Grey	Beige	EL1372	1377	
1950		Grey	Red	EL1373	1378	
1950		UNP	Red	EL1374	1375	
1950	Buckl			EL1375	1362	
1950		Black	Red	EL1376	1379	
1950		Grey	Red	EL1377	1380	
1950		Black	Red	EL1378	1383	
1950		Grey	Blue	EL1379	1384	
1950		Grey	Blue	EL1380	1386	
1950		Blue	Blue	EL1381	1387	
1950	Buckl			EL1382	1371	
1950		UNP	Blue	EL1383	1385	
1950		Blue	Blue	EL1384	1388	
1950		Black	Beige	EL1385	1389	
1950	Buckl			EL1386	1372	
1950		Grey	Beige	EL1387	1390	
1950		Black	Beige	EL1388	1391	
1950		Grey	Beige	EL1389	1392	
1950		Black	Red	EL1390	1393	
1950		Black	Beige	EL1391	1394	
1950		Grey	Red	EL1392	1395	
1950	Buckl			EL1393	N/A	
1950		Grey	Red	EL1394	1396	
1950		Grey	Blue	EL1395	1397	
1950		Grey	Red	EL1396	1398	
1950		Grey	Red	EL1397	1399	
1950		Grey	Blue	EL1398	1400	
1950		Grey	Blue	EL1399	1401	
1950		Grey	Blue	EL1400	1402	Belfast
1950		Black	Beige	EL1401	1403	
1950		Black	Beige	EL1402	1404	
1950	Buckl			EL1403	1382	
1950		Grey	N/A	EL1404	N/A	
1950		Black	Beige	EL1405	1406	
1950		Grey	Red	EL1406	1407	
1950		Grey	Beige	EL1407	1408	
1950		Grey	Red	EL1408	1409	
N/A		N/A	N/A	EL1409	N/A	
1950		UNP	Red	EL1410	1413	
1950		Grey	Red	EL1411	1414	
1950		Blue	Blue	EL1412	1415	
1950		UNP	Blue	EL1413	1416	
1950		Grey	Blue	EL1414	1417	
1950		Grey	Blue	EL1415	1418	
1950		Grey	Beige	EL1416	1419	
1950		Blue	Blue	EL1417	1420	
1950		Black	Beige	EL1418	1421	
N/A	Buckl	N/A	N/A	ELX1419	N/A	
1950		Grey	Beige	EL1420	1423	
1950		Grey	Blue	EL1421	1422	
1950		Grey	Beige	EL1422	1424	
1950		Grey	Beige	EL1423	1426	
1950	Buckl	N/A	N/A	EL1424	1410	
1950		Black	Red	EL1425	1425	
1950		Grey	Red	ELX1426	1428	Montevideo
1950		Black	Red	EL1427	1429	
1950		Grey	Red	EL1428	1431	
1950		Grey	Red	EL1429	1432	
1950		Grey	Blue	EL1430	1430	
1950		Grey	Blue	EL1431	1433	
1950	Buckl	N/A	N/A	EL1432	1427	
1950		Grey	Blue	EL1433	1435	
N/A		N/A	N/A	1434	N/A	
1950		Grey	Blue	EL1435	1437	
1950		Grey	Beige	EL1436	1438	
1950	Buckl	N/A	N/A	EL1437	1434	
1950		Grey	Beige	EL1438	1440	

First reg	Body type	Body colour	Interior colour	Chassis no.	Engine no.	Comments
1950		Black	Beige	EL1439	1374	
1950		Grey	Beige	EL1440	1441	
1950		Grey	Beige	EL1441	1442	
1950		Black	Red	EL1442	1443	
1950		Black	Red	EL1443	1444	
1950		Grey	Red	EL1444	1445	
1950		Beige	Red	EL1445	N/A	Brochure car
1950		UNP	Blue	EL1446	1447	
N/A		N/A	N/A	1447	N/A	
1950		Grey	Blue	EL1448	N/A	
1950		Grey	Blue	EL1449	N/A	
1950		Blue	Blue	EL1450	1451	
1950		Grey	Blue	EL1451	1452	
1950		Grey	Beige	EL1452	1451	
1950		Black	Beige	EL1453	1453	
1950		N/A	N/A	EL1454	1455	
1950		Black	Beige	EL1455	1456	Belfast
1950		Grey	Red	EL1456	1457	
1950		Black	Beige	EL1457	1458	
1950		Grey	Red	EL1458	1459	
1950		Grey	Red	1459	N/A	
1950		Grey	Red	1460	1461	
1950		Black	Red	1461	1462	
1950		Grey	Blue	1462	N/A	
1950	Buckl	N/A	N/A	EL1463	1469	
1950	Buckl	N/A	N/A	EL1464	1466	
1950	Buckl	N/A	N/A	EL1465	1470	
1950		Blue	Blue	1466	N/A	
1950		N/A	N/A	EL1467	1465	
1950		Grey	Blue	1468	1467	
1950		Grey	Beige	EL1469	1468	
1950		Grey	Blue	1470	1471	
1950		Grey	Beige	1471	1472	
1950		Black	Beige	EL1472	1473	
1950		UNP	N/A	1473	1474	
1950		Black	Beige	1474	1475	
1950		Grey	Red	1475	1476	
1950		Grey	Beige	1476	1477	
1950		Black	Red	EL1477	1478	
1950	Buckl			EL1478	1481	
1950		Black	Red	EL1479	1479	
1950		Grey	Blue	1480	1480	
1950		Black	Red	1481	1482	
1950		Grey	Blue	EL1482	1483	
1950	Buckl			EL1483	1484	
1950		Grey	Blue	EL1484	1485	
1950		Blue	Blue	1485	1486	
1950		UNP	Blue	EL1486	1487	
1950		Green	Beige	EL1487	1488	
1950	Buckl			EL1488	1489	
1950		N/A	N/A	EL1489	1490	
1950		N/A	N/A	1490	1491	
1950		Grey	Beige	1491	1492	
1950		Black	Beige	EL1492	1493	
1950		Black	Red	EL1493	1494	
1950	Buckl			EL1494	N/A	
1950		Grey	Red	EL1495	1495	
1950		Black	Red	EL1496	1497	
1950		Grey	Blue	EL1497	1498	
1950		UNP	N/A	EL1498	1499	
1950		Beige	Red	EL1499	1500	
1950		Grey	Blue	EL1500	1502	
1950		Grey	Blue	EL1501	1501	
1950		Grey	Blue	EL1502	1503	
1950	Buckl	N/A	N/A	EL1503	1504	
1950		Grey	Red	EL1504	1505	
1950		Grey	Blue	EL1505	1506	
1950		Black	Red	EL1506	1507	
1950		N/A	N/A	EL1507	1509	
1950		Grey	Red	EL1508	1510	
1950		Black	Red	EL1509	1511	Belfast
1950		Black	Beige	EL1510	1514	
1950		Grey	Red	EL1511	1512	
1950	Buckl	N/A	N/A	ELX1512	1508	USA
1950		Grey	Red	EL1513	1513	
1950		Grey	Red	EL1514	1515	
1950		Grey	Red	EL1515	1516	
1950		Grey	Blue	EL1516	1517	
1950		Grey	Blue	EL1517	1519	
1950		Black	Red	EL1518	1520	
1950		Grey	Beige	EL1519	1522	
1950		Blue	Blue	EL1520	1518	
1950		Grey	N/A	EL1521	1525	Nairobi?
1950		Grey	Blue	EL1522	1521	

First reg	Body type	Body colour	Interior colour	Chassis no.	Engine no.	Comments
1950		Grey	Beige	ELX1523	1523	
1950		Grey	Beige	EL1524	1524	
1950	Buckl	N/A	N/A	EL1525	1526	
1950		Grey	Red	EL1526	1527	
1950		Black	Red	EL1527	1529	
1950		Black	Beige	EL1528	1528	
1950		Black	Red	EL1529	1530	
1950		Black	Red	EL1530	1531	
1950		Grey	Red	EL1531	1532	
1950		Grey	Beige	EL1532	1533	
1950		Grey	Blue	EL1533	1534	
1950	Buckl	N/A	N/A	EL1534	1535	
1950		Grey	Blue	EL1535	1536	
1950		Grey	N/A	EL1536	1537	
1950	Buckl	NA/	N/A	EL1537	1538	
1950		Grey	Blue	EL1538	1539	
1950		Grey	Blue	EL1539	1540	
1950		N/A	N/A	EL1540	1541	
1950		Black	Beige	EL1541	1542	
1950		Grey	Beige	EL1542	1543	
1950		Black	Beige	EL1543	1544	
1950		Black	Red	EL1544	1545	
1950		Grey	Red	EL1545	1546	
1950		Black	Red	EL1546	1547	
1950		Black	Red	EL1547	1548	
1950		Grey	Blue	EL1548	1549	
N/A		N/A	N/A	EL1549	N/A	
1950	Buckl	N/A	N/A	EL1550	1552	
N/A		N/A	N/A	EL1551	N/A	
N/A		Grey	Blue	EL1552	1554	
N/A		Grey	Blue	EL1553	1550	
1950		Grey	Blue	EL1554	N/A	
1950		Black	Beige	EL1555	1556	
1950		Blue	Beige	EL1556	1591	Built for C Hurlock
1950	Buckl	N/A	N/A	EL1557	1558	
1951		Black	Beige	EL1558	1559	
1951		Grey	Beige	EL1559	1560	
1951		Grey	Red	EL1560	1561	
1951		N/A	Beige	EL1561	1564	
1951		N/A	N/A	EL1562	1566	
1951		Beige	Red	EL1563	1567	
1950	Buckl	N/A	N/A	EL1564	1568	
1951		Grey	Blue	EL1565	1562	
1951		Grey	Red	EL1566	1563	
1951		Grey	Blue	EL1567	1565	
1951		Black	Red	EL1568	1569	
1951		Grey	Blue	EL1569	1570	
1951		Grey	Blue	EL1570	1571	
1951		Grey	Beige	EL1571	1572	
1951		Grey	Blue	EL1572	1574	
1950	Buckl	N/A	N/A	EL1573	1573	
1951		Black	Beige	EL1574	1575	
1951		Black	Beige	EL1575	1576	Belfast
1951		N/A	N/A	EL1576	1577	
1951		Grey	Beige	EL1577	1582	
1951		N/A	N/A	EL1578	N/A	
1951		N/A	N/A	EL1579	1579	
1950	Buckl	N/A	N/A	EL1580	1578	
1951		Black	Red	EL1581	N/A	
1951		Grey	Red	EL1582	1583	
1951		Black	Red	EL1583	1584	
1951		Grey	Blue	EL1584	1585	
1951		Grey	Blue	EL1585	1586	
1951		Grey	Blue	EL1586	1587	
1951		Black	Beige	EL1587	N/A	
1951		Blue	Blue	EL1588	1588	
1951		Grey	Blue	EL1589	1589	
1951		Black	Beige	EL1590	1590	
1950	Buckl	N/A	N/A	EL1591	1592	
1951		Grey	Beige	EL1592	1593	
1951		N/A	N/A	EL1593	1595	
1951		Grey	Red	EL1594	1596	
1951		Grey	Beige	EL1595	1597	
1951		Grey	Beige	EL1596	N/A	
1951		N/A	N/A	EL1597	1601	
1951		Black	Red	EL1598	1602	
1951		Grey	Blue	EL1599	1603	
1951		Grey	Blue	EL1600	1604	
1951		Grey	Blue	EL1601	1605	
N/A		Beige	Red	EL1602	N/A	Belgium
1950	Buckl	N/A	N/A	ELX1603	1600	
1951		N/A	N/A	EL1604	1606	
1951		Grey	Blue	EL1605	1607	

First reg	Body type	Body colour	Interior colour	Chassis no.	Engine no.	Comments
1951		Grey	Beige	EL1606	1608	
1951	Buckl	NA/	N/A	EL1607	1598	
1951		Black	Beige	EL1608	1609	
1951		Black	Beige	EL1609	1600	
1951		Black	Beige	EL1610	1611	
1951		Grey	Beige	EL1611	1612	
1951		Grey	Red	EL1612	N/A	
1951		Beige	Red	EL1613	1614	
1951	Buckl	N/A	N/A	EL1614	1615	
1951		Grey	Red	EL1615	1616	
1951		Black	Red	EL1616	1618	
1951		Grey	Blue	EL1617	1617	
1951		Grey	Blue	EL1618	N/A	
1951		Grey	Blue	EL1619	1621	
1951		Blue	Blue	EL1620	1633	
1951		Grey	Beige	EL1621	1622	
1951		Grey	Blue	EL1622	1624	
1951		Grey	Blue	EL1623	N/A	
1951		Grey	Beige	EL1624	1623	
1951		Grey	Red	EL1625	N/A	
1951	Buckl	N/A	N/A	EL1626	1630	
1951		Green	Beige	EL1627	1626	Built for W Hurlock
1951		Green	Beige	EL1628	1627	
1951		Grey	Beige	EL1629	1628	
1951		Black	Red	EL1630	1629	
N/A		N/A	N/A	EL1631	N/A	
1951	Buckl	N/A	N/A	EL1632	1632	
1951		N/A	N/A	EL1633	1635	
1951		Black	Red	EL1634	N/A	
1951		Grey	Blue	EL1635	1636	
1951		Black	Red	EL1636	1637	
1951		Blue	Blue	EL1637	1638	
1951		Grey	Blue	EL1638	1639	
1951		Black	Beige	EL1639	1640	
1951	Buckl	N/A	N/A	EL1640	1641	
1951		Grey	Blue	EL1641	1642	
1951		Grey	Beige	EL1642	1643	
1951		Black	Beige	EL1643	N/A	
1951		Black	Beige	EL1644	1646	
1951		Grey	Beige	EL1645	1645	
1951	Buckl	N/A	N/A	EL1646	1647	
1951		Grey	Red	EL1647	1648	
1951		Black	Red	EL1648	1649	
1951		Black	Red	EL1649	1650	
1951		Black	Red	EL1650	1651	
1951		Grey	Blue	EL1651	1652	
N/A		N/A	N/A	EL1652	N/A	
1951		Beige	Red	EL1653	1654	
1951	Buckl	N/A	N/A	EL1654	1655	
1951		Beige	Red	EL1655	1656	
1951		Blue	Blue	EL1656	1657	
1951		Grey	Blue	EL1657	1658	
N/A		N/A	N/A	EL1658	N/A	
N/A		Green	Beige	EL1659	1660	Built for Mr Sidney (AC Cars)
1951		Green	Beige	EL1660	1661	
1951	Buckl	N/A	N/A	EL1661	1662	
1951		Black	Beige	EL1662	1663	
1951		Grey	Blue	EL1663	1664	
1951		Grey	Beige	EL1664	1665	New Zealand
1951		Black	Red	EL1665	1666	
1951		Black	Red	EL1666	1667	New Zealand
1951		Blue	Blue	EL1667	1668	New Zealand
1951	Buckl	N/A	N/A	EL1668	1671	
1951		Grey	Blue	EL1669	1672	
1951		Blue	Blue	EL1670	1673	
1951		Grey	Blue	EL1671	1674	
1951		Black	Red	ELX1672	1669	
1951		Black	Red	ELX1673	1670	
1951		Grey	Blue	EL1674	1675	
1951	Buckl	N/A	N/A	EL1675	1675	S/B UMB 1676?
1951		Grey	Beige	EL1676	1677	
1951		Grey	Beige	EL1677	1678	
1951		Grey	Beige	EL1678	1679	
N/A		N/A	N/A	EL1679	1680	
1951		N/A	N/A	EL1680	1681	
1951		Grey	Blue	EL1681	1682	
1951	Buckl	N/A	N/A	EL1682	1683	1 piece front?
1951		Grey	Blue	EL1683	1684	
1951		Grey	Blue	EL1684	1685	
1951		Grey	Blue	EL1685	1686	

First reg	Body type	Body colour	Interior colour	Chassis no.	Engine no.	Comments
1951		Grey	Blue	EL1686	1687	
1951		Grey	Blue	EL1687	1688	
1951		Grey	Blue	EL1688	1689	
1951		Black	Beige	EL1689	1699	
1951		Grey	Beige	EL1701	1701	
1951		Grey	Beige	EL1702	1703	
1951		Blue	Blue	EL1703	1704	
1951		Black	Red	EL1704	1705	
1951		Black	Red	EL1705	1706	
1951		Grey	Red	EL1706	1707	
1951	Buckl	N/A	N/A	EL1707	1708	
1951		Black	Red	EL1708	1709	
N/A		N/A	N/A	EL1709	1710	
1951	Buckl	N/A	N/A	EL1710	1711	
1951		Grey	Red	EL1711	1712	
1951		N/A	N/A	EL1712	1713	
1951		Beige	Red	EL1713	1714	
1951		Black	Red	EL1714	1715	
1951		Black	Red	EL1715	1716	
1951	Buckl	N/A	N/A	EL1716	1717	
1951		Grey	Blue	EL1717	1718	
1951		Grey	Blue	EL1718	1719	
1951		Grey	Blue	EL1719	1720	
1951		Grey	Blue	EL1720	1722	
1951		Grey	Blue	EL1721	1722	
1951		Grey	Blue	EL1722	1723	
1951	Buckl	N/A	N/A	EL1723	1724	
1951		Blue	Blue	EL1724	1725	
1951		Blue	Blue	EL1725	1726	
1951		Grey	Blue	EL1726	1727	
1951		Grey	Blue	EL1727	1728	
N/A		N/A	N/A	EL1728	N/A	
1951		Black	Beige	EL1729	1730	
1951	Buckl	N/A	N/A	EL1730	1731	
N/A		N/A	N/A	EL1731	N/A	
1951		Grey	Beige	EL1732	1733	
1951		Black	Beige	EL1733	1734	
N/A		Black	Beige	EL1734	1735	
N/A	Buckl	N/A	N/A	EL1735	1736	
1951		Grey	Beige	EL1736	1737	
1951		Grey	Beige	EL1737	N/A	
N/A		Green	Beige	EL1738	1738	

First reg	Body type	Body colour	Interior colour	Chassis no.	Engine no.	Comments
1951		Black	Beige	EL1739	1740	
1951		Grey	Red	EL1740	1741	
1951	Buckl	N/A	N/A	EL1741	1742	
N/A		N/A	N/A	EL1742	N/A	
1951		Black	Red	EL1743	1744	
1951		N/A	N/A	EL1744	1745	
N/A		Black	Red	EL1745	1746	AC Cars demo?
1951		Grey	Red	EL1746	1747	
1951	Buckl	N/A	N/A	EL1747	1749	
N/A		N/A	N/A	EL1748	N/A	
1951		Black	Red	1749	1750	
1951		Black	Red	1750	1751	
1951		Black	Red	EL1751	1752	
1951		Grey	Blue	EL1752	1753	
1951		Black	Beige	EL1753	1754	
1951		Blue	Blue	EL1754	1755	
1951		Grey	Blue	EL1755	1755?	
N/A		Black	Beige	EL1756	1758	
1951		Grey	Blue	EL1757	1759	
1951		Blue	Blue	EL1758	1760	
1951		Grey	Blue	1759	1761	
1951		Blue	Blue	EL1760	1762	
N/A		Grey	Blue	EL1761	1763	
1951		Grey	Blue	EL1762	1764	
1951		Green	Beige	EL1763	1765	
1951		Black	Beige	EL1764	1766	Belfast
1951		Grey	Beige	EL1765	1767	
1951		Grey	Beige	EL1766	1768	
1951		Black	Beige	EL1767	1769	
1951		Black	Beige	1768	1770	
1951		Black	Beige	EL1769	1771	
1951		Green	Beige	EL1770	1774	
1951		Black	Beige	EL1771	1775	
1951		Beige	Red	EL1772	1776	
1951		Beige	Red	EL1773	1777	
1951		Black	Red	EL1774	1778	
1951	?	N/A	N/A	ELX1775	1772	Denmark
1951	?	N/A	N/A	ELX1776	N/A	Denmark
1951		Green	Red	EL1777	1779	
1951		Black	Red	EL1778	1757	
1951		Black	Red	EL1779	1780	

First reg	Body type	Body colour	Interior colour	Chassis no.	Engine no.	Comments
1951		Grey	Red	EL1780	1781	
1951		Grey	Red	EL1781	1782	AC Cars demo?
1951		Black	Red	EL1782	1783	
1951		Black	Red	EL1783	1785	
1951		Grey	Blue	1784	1786	
1951		Grey	Blue	EL1785	1784	
1951		Grey	Blue	EL1786	1787	
1951		Grey	Blue	EL1787	1788	
1951		Grey	Blue	1788	1789	
1951		Grey	Blue	EL1789	1790	
1951		Grey	Blue	EL1790	1792	
1951		Grey	Blue	1791	1791	
1951	Buckl	N/A	N/A	EL1792	1793	
1951		Grey	Blue	EL1793	1794	
1951		Grey	Blue	1794	1795	
1951		Grey	Beige	EL1795	1796	
1951		Black	Beige	EL1796	1797	
N/A		Black	Beige	EL1797	1798	
N/A		Black	Beige	EL1798	1799	
N/A		Grey	Beige	EL1799	N/A	
1951		Black	Beige	EL1800	1801	
1951		Black	Beige	EL1801	1806	
1951		Blue	Beige	EL1802	1805	
1951		Grey	Beige	EL1803	1802	
1951		Black	Beige	EL1804	1803	
1951		Black	Red	EL1805	1807	
1951		Grey	Red	EH1806	1804	
1951		Grey	Red	EH1807	1808	
1951		Black	Red	EH1808	1809	
1951		Black	Red	EH1809	1810	
1951	4D			EH1810	N/A	First 4 door
1951		Black	Red	EH1811	1812	
1951	Buckl	N/A	N/A	EL1812	1813	
1951		Black	Red	EH1813	1814	
N/A		Black	Beige	EH1814	N/A	
1951		Black	Red	EH1815	1816	
1951		Blue	Blue	EH1816	1817	
1951		Grey	Blue	EH1817	1818	
1951		Grey	Blue	EH1818	1819	
1951		Grey	Blue	EH1819	1820	
1951		Grey	Blue	EH1820	1821	
1951		Grey	Blue	EH1821	1822	
1951		Blue	Blue	EH1822	1823	
N/A		Grey	Blue	EH1823	1824	
1952		Blue	Blue	EH1824	1826	
N/A		N/A	N/A	EH1825	N/A	
1951		Black	Beige	EH1826	1829	
1951		Black	Beige	EH1827	1828	
1951?		N/A	N/A	EH1828	1829	
1951		Green	Beige	EH1829	1830	Spain
1951		N/A	N/A	EH1830	1831	
1951		Black	Beige	EH1831	1832	
1951		Black	Beige	EH1832	N/A	
N/A		Green	N/A	EH1833	N/A	
1951		Black	Beige	EH1834	1836	
1952		Grey	Beige	EH1835	1837	
1952		Grey	Beige	EH1836	N/A	
1951		Black	Red	EH1837	1839	
1951	Buckl	N/A	N/A	EH1838	1835	
N/A		Grey	Red	EH1938	1841	
1952		Beige	Red	EH1840	1842	
1951		N/A	Red	EH1841	1843	
1951		Black	Red	EH1842	1845	
1952		Black	Red	EH1843	1844	
N/A		Grey	Red	EH1844	1846	
1952		Grey	Red	EH1845	1847	
1952		Green	Red	EH1846	1840	
1952	Buckl	N/A	N/A	EH1847	N/A	
1952		Grey	Blue	EH1848	1849	
1952		Grey	Blue	EH1849	1851	
1952		Grey	Blue	EH1850	1852	
1952		Blue	Blue	EH1851	1850	
1952		Grey	Blue	EH1852	1853	
1952		Grey	Blue	EH1853	1854	
1952		Grey	Blue	EH1854	1855	AC Cars demo?
1952		Grey	Blue	EH1855	1857	
N/A	Buckl	N/A	N/A	EH1856	1856	
1952		Grey	Blue	EH1857	1858	
1952		Grey	Beige	EH1858	1859	
1952		Black	Beige	EH1859	1860	
1952		Green	Beige	EH1860	1861	Isle of Man
1952		Grey	Beige	EH1861	1862	

First reg	Body type	Body colour	Interior colour	Chassis no.	Engine no.	Comments	First reg	Body type	Body colour	Interior colour	Chassis no.	Engine no.	Comments
952		Black	Beige	EH1862	1863		1952		Black	Red	EH1902	1904	
952		Grey	Beige	EH1863	1864		1952		Grey	Red	EH1903	1905	
952		Black	Beige	EH1864	1867		1952		Black	Red	EH1904	1904	
952		Green	Beige	EH1865	1866		1952		Black	Red	EH1905	1907	
952		Black	Beige	EH1866	1865		1952		Black	Red	EH1906	1909	
952		Green	Beige	EH1867	1868	AC Cars demo?	1952		Beige	Red	EH1907	1908	
							1952		Grey	Blue	EH1908	1911	
952		Black	Red	EH1868	1869		1952	Buckl	N/A	N/A	EH1909	1910	
952		Beige	Red	EH1869	1870		1952		Beige	Red	EH1910	1912	
952		Black	Red	EH1870	1871		1952	Buckl	Grey	Blue	EH1911	1913	
952		Black	Red	EH1871	1872		1952		Grey	Blue	EH1912	1914	
952		Grey	Red	EH1872	1873	AC Cars demo?	1952		Blue	Red	EH1913	1915	
							1952		Grey	Blue	EH1914	1916	
951		Grey	Red	EH1873	1874	Jersey	1952		Grey	Blue	EH1915	1917	
952		N/A	N/A	EH1874	1875		1952		Grey	Blue	EH1916	1919	
952		Beige	Red	EH1875	1877	Jersey	1952		Blue	Blue	EH1917	1920	
952		Grey	Red	EH1876	1876		1952		Blue	Blue	EH1918	1918	
952		Beige	Red	EH1877	1878		1952		Black	Beige	EH1919	N/A	Seychelles?
952		Grey	Blue	EH1878	1880		1952		Black	Beige	EH1920	1922	
952		Blue	Blue	EH1879	1881		1952		Blue	Blue	EH1921	1923	
952		Grey	Blue	EH1880	1882		1952		Green	Beige	EH1922	1924	
952		Blue	Blue	EH1881	1883		1952		Grey	Beige	EH1923	1925	
952		Grey	Blue	EH1882	1884		1952		Green	Beige	EH1924	1926	
952		N/A	N/A	EH1883	1885		1952		Blue	Beige	EH1925	1927	Sweden?
952		Grey	N/A	EH1884	1886		1952		Grey	Beige	EH1926	1929	Jersey?
952		Grey	Blue	EH1885	1887		1952		Black	Beige	EH1927	1930	
952		N/A	N/A	EH1886	1888		1952		Beige	Red	EH1928	1928	
952		Grey	Red	EH1887	1889		1952		Grey	Beige	EH1929	1931	Ceylon?
952		N/A	N/A	1888	N/A	Belfast	1952		UNP	Beige	EH1930	N/A	
952		Grey	Beige	EH1889	1891		1952		Grey	Red	EH1931	1933	Kenya
952		Grey	Blue	EH1890	1892		1952		Black	Red	EH1932	N/A	
952		Black	Beige	EH1891	1893		1952	Tourer?	N/A	N/A	EH1933	N/A	
952		Black	Beige	EH1892	1894		1952		Grey	Red	EH1934	1936	
952		Beige	Beige	EH1893	1895		1952		Grey	Red	EH1935	1937	
952	Buckl	Green	Beige	EH1894	1896		1952		Black	Red	EH1936	1938	
952		N/A	N/A	EH1895	1897		1952		Black	Red	EH1937	1939	
952		Black	Beige	EH1896	1898		1952		Black	Red	EH1938	1940	
N/A		Blue	Blue	EH1897	N/A		N/A	?	N/A	N/A	EH1939	N/A	AC Cars demo
952		Black	Beige	EH1898	1920								
N/A		N/A	N/A	1899			1952		Black	Red	EH1940	1942	
952		Grey	Blue	EH1900	1902		1952		Grey	Blue	EH1941	1943	
952		Grey	Red	EH1901	1903		1952		Grey	Blue	EH1942	1944	

First reg	Body type	Body colour	Interior colour	Chassis no.	Engine no.	Comments
1952		Grey	Blue	EH1943	1945	
1952		Blue	Blue	EH1944	1946	
1952		Grey	Blue	EH1945	1947	
1952		Grey	Blue	EH1946	1948	
1953		Grey	Blue	EH1947	1949	
1953		Grey	Blue	EH1948	1951	AC Cars
1953		Grey	Blue	EH1949	1950	
1953		Grey	Blue	EH1950	1952	
1952		Black	Beige	EH1951	1954	
1952		Green	Beige	EH1952	1955	
1952		Black	Beige	EH1953	1953	
N/A		N/A	N/A	EH1954	N/A	Cut down chassis
1953		Black	Beige	EH1955	1956	
N/A		Green	Beige	EH1956	1958	
1952		Grey	Beige	EH1957	1957	
1952		Grey	Beige	EH1958	1959	
1953		Black	Beige	EH1959	1960	
1952		Black	Beige	EH1960	1961	
1953		Grey	Beige	EH1961	1962	AC Cars
1952		Black	Red	EH1962	1963	
N/A		Black	Red	EH1963	1966	
1952	Buckl?	N/A	N/A	EH1964	1964	
1952		Black	Red	EH1965	1965	
1953		Grey	Red	EH1966	1967	
1952		Beige	Red	EH1967	1968	
1952		Grey	Red	EH1968	1969	
1952		Black	Red	EH1969	1970	
1953		Black	Red	EH1970	1971	
1952		Blue	Blue	EH1971	1972	Jersey
1952		Black	Red	EH1972	1973	
1953		Blue	Blue	EH1973	1975	
1953		Grey	Blue	EH1974	1974	W Hurlock
1952		Black	Red	EH1975	1976	
1952	2L SP T	Buckl	N/A	EH1976	N/A	Buck/style
1953		Blue	Blue	EH1977	1977	
1953		Green	Beige	EH1978	1979	
1953		Green	Beige	EH1979	1980	
1952		Blue	Blue	EH1980	1981	
1953		Grey	Beige	EH1981	1982	
1953		Black	Beige	EH1982	1983	
1952		Beige	Red	EH1983	1984	
1952	2L SP T		N/A	EH1984	1986	Buck/style
1952		Beige	Red	EH1985	1985	
1952		Beige	Red	EH1986	1988	
1952		Beige	Red	EH1987	1990	
1952	2L SP T	N/A	N/A	EH1988	1991	Buck/style
1952		Grey	Blue	EH1989	1992	
1953		Blue	Blue	EH1990	1993	
1953		Beige	Red	EH1991	1994	Latest pattern trimming
1953		Blue	Blue	EH1992	1989	
1953		Green	Beige	EH1993	1995	
1953		Blue	Blue	EH1994	1996	
1953		Beige	Beige	EH1995	1998	
1953		Black	Red	EH1996	1987	
1953		Green	Beige	EH1997	1997	
1953		Grey	Beige	EH1998	1879?	
1953		Blue	Beige	EH1999	1999	
1953		Beige	Red	EH2000	2000	
1953		Beige	Red	EH2001	2004	
1953		Green	Beige	EH2002	2002	
1952	2L SP T	N/A	N/A	EH2003	2001	Buck/style
1953		Beige	Red	EH2004	2005	
1953		Black	Beige	EH2005	2003	
1953		Peony	Grey	EH2006	N/A	
1953		Grey	Red	EH2007	2007	
1953		Black	Beige	EH2008	2008	
1953		Beige	Red	EH2009	2009	
1954		Green	Beige	EH2010	2011	
1954		Black	Beige	EH2011	2012	
1954		Blue	Beige	EH2012	2098	
1954		Green	Beige	EH2013	2015	
1954		Green	Beige	EH2014	2016	
1955		Beige	Red	EH2015	2017	
1954		Grey	Red	EH2016	2076	
1954		Beige	Red	EH2017	2018	Owned by Rivers Fletcher
1954		Beige	Beige	EH2018	2019	
1953	DHC	Grey	Beige	EH2019	2010	Motor Show car (twin petrol tanks)

First reg	Body type	Body colour	Interior colour	Chassis no.	Engine no.	Comments
1952	4DR	Blue	Beige	EH2020	2026	Start of 4 door production
N/A	4DR	Blue	Beige	EHX2021	2022	
N/A	4DR	Black	Beige	EHX2022	2023	
1953	4DR	Green	Beige	EH2023	2024	
1953	4DR	Blue	Blue	EH2024	2025	AC Cars demo?
1953	4DR	Black	Beige	EH2025	2020	
1953	4DR	Green	Beige	EH2026	2027	
1953		Beige	Red	EHX2027	2028	LHD
1953	4DR	Black	Beige	EH2028	2030	
1953	4DR	Beige	Red	EH2029	2029	
1953	4DR	Green	Beige	EH2030	2031	
1953	2L SP T	Ivory	Red	EH2031	2021	Buck/style
1953		Green	Beige	EH2032	2032	
1953	4DR	Grey	Red	EH2033	2033	Two-tone paintwork
1953	2L SP T	Grey	Red	EHX2034	2041	Buck/style
1953	4DR	Blue	Beige	EH2035	2034	Japan
1953	Buckl	N/A	N/A	EH2036	2035	
1953	4DR	Green	Beige	EH2037	2036	
1953	2L SP T	Green	Green	EH2038	2051	Buck/style
1953	2L SP T	Blue	Grey	EH2039	2054	Buck/style
1953	2L SP T	Black	Red	EH2040	2053	Buck/style
1953	2L SP T	Black	Red	EH2041	2055	Buck/style
1953	2L SP T	White	Red	EH2042	2057	Buck/style
1953	2L SP T	Ivory	Red	EHX2043	2048	Buck/style
1953	2L SP T	Opaline	Beige	EHX2044	2047	Buck/style
1955	4DR	Blue	Blue	EH2045	2080	Belfast
1954	4DR	Green	Beige	EH2046	2040	
1953	4DR	Green	Beige	EH2047	2037	
1953	4DR	Green	Beige	EH2048	2038	
1953	4DR	Green	Beige	EH2049	2039	
1953	4DR	Green	Beige	EH2050	2042	
1953	2L SP T	Maroon	Maroon	EH2051	2045	Buck/style
1954	?	Black	Red	EH2052	2061	
1954	4DR	Black	Red	EH2053	2050	
1954	4DR	Green	Red	EH2054	2059	
1954	2L SP T	White	White	EH2055	2058	Buck/style
1954	4DR	Black	Beige	EH2056	2062	
1954	4DR	Grey	Beige	EH2057	2064	

First reg	Body type	Body colour	Interior colour	Chassis no.	Engine no.	Comments
1954	4DR	Green	Beige	EH2058	2065	
1954	4DR	Blue	Beige	EH2059	2066	
1954	2L SP T	Black	Red	EH2060	2049	Buck/style
1954	4DR	Green	Beige	EH2061	2067	
1954	4DR	Grey	Beige	EH2062	2074	
1954	4DR	Green	Beige	EH2063	2072	
1954	4DR	Blue	Blue	EH2064	2071	
1954	4DR	Beige	Blue	EH2065	2075	
1954	4DR	Grey	Red	EH2066	2073	
1954	4DR	Grey	Red	EH2067	2078	
1954	4DR	Green	Beige	EH2068	2014	
1954	4DR	Ivory	Green	EH2069	2091	Pacific Green wings
1955	4DR	Blue	Beige	EH2070	2092	
1954		Ivory	Blue	EH2071	2013	
1954	4DR	Ivory/ Red	Red	EH2072	2103	
1955	4DR	Black	Beige	EH2073	2052	
1955	4DR	Green	Beige	EH2074	2105	
1954	4DR	Grey/ Damson	Red	EH2075	2108	
1955		Beige	Beige	EH2076	2109	
1955		Green	Beige	EH2077	2111	
1955	4DR	Blue	Beige	EH2078	2110	
1955	4DR	Blue	Beige	EH2079	2112	
1955		Green	Ivory/ Green	EH2080	2088	
1955	4DR	Green	Red	EH2081	2138	
1955		Black	Red	EH2082	CL2150	
1955		Green	Beige	EH2083	N/A	
1955	4DR	Black	Red	EH2084	2138	France
1955	4DR	Green	Beige	EH2085	2181	
1955		Black	Beige	EH2086	CL2186	
1956	4DR	Black	Red	EH2087	CL2201	
1956	4DR	Green	Beige	EH2088	2088	
1955		Blue	Blue	EH2089	CL2216	
1956		Blue	Beige	EH2090	N/A	
1956		Black	Red	EHX2091	N/A	USA
1956		Black	Beige	EH2092	CL2247	
1957	4DR	Black	Beige	EH2093	CL2255	
1958		Green	Beige	EH2094	CL2343	
1958		Blue	Blue	EH2095	CL2365	Last saloon

INDEX

Visit Veloce on the web - **www.veloce.co.uk**